"[A] compelling mix of memoir and reporting."

—*O, The Oprah Magazine*

"Unforgettable . . . Carvajal immerses herself and her readers in the ringing of Arcos's ancient bells, the stories of its town historian, or *cronista*, and, most of all, the performance of haunting religious songs known as *saetas* that may have originated as Jewish laments."

—*Chicago Tribune*

"This book is an important addition to the record of Jewish history, not because it describes what history books already can tell us but because it evokes a personal sense of both loss and redemption growing out of that brutal history."

—*The Kansas City Star*

"Darkly poetic."

—*The Christian Science Monitor*

"Carvajal is a journalist who understands the nuance and beauty of travel writing. Combining this gift with this highly personal story, she creates a book that shimmers with enchantment, pulling the reader into her life with gentle tugs on the heartstrings. What she calls 'hunting family ghosts' will resonate with anyone who has ever felt out of place where they were and dreamed of finding another heritage just one layer beneath the one they had always accepted as the bedrock of their self-definition."

—Jewish Book Council

continued . . .

"A mesmerizing journey through time, across cultures, and into one woman's rich personal history."

"A cohesive and engaging narrative of self-discovery and historical investigation."

"Such an intriguing topic, and Carvajal . . . certainly knows how to write."

"[Carvajal's] exploration reveals the fascinating legacy of the Jewish *conversos* . . . Her experiences not only reflect a heartfelt attempt to recapture a lost identity but also serve as a launching point for a wider exploration of the repercussions of the Inquisition."

"Doreen Carvajal has undertaken an extraordinary journey, and the story she tells is both personal and universal."

The Forgetting River

A MODERN TALE OF SURVIVAL, IDENTITY, AND THE INQUISITION

DOREEN CARVAJAL

RIVERHEAD BOOKS
New York

RIVERHEAD BOOKS
Published by the Penguin Group
Penguin Group (USA) Inc.
375 Hudson Street, New York, New York 10014, USA

USA | Canada | UK | Ireland | Australia | New Zealand | India | South Africa | China

Penguin Books Ltd., Registered Offices: 80 Strand, London WC2R 0RL, England
For more information about the Penguin Group, visit penguin.com.

The Library of Congress has catalogued the Riverhead hardcover edition as follows:

Carvajal, Doreen.
The forgetting river : a modern tale of survival, identity, and
the Inquisition / Doreen Carvajal.
p.   cm.
ISBN 978-1-59448-739-2
1. Jews—Spain—Arcos de la Frontera.   2. Crypto-Jews—Spain—
Arcos de la Frontera.   3. Marranos—Arcos de la Frontera.
4. Inquisition—Spain.   5. Arcos de la Frontera (Spain)—Description and travel.
6. Carvajal, Doreen—Travel.   I. Title.
DS135.S75A84   2012   2012009180
305.892'404688—dc23

First Riverhead hardcover edition: August 2012
First Riverhead trade paperback edition: August 2013
Riverhead trade paperback ISBN: 978-1-59463-152-8

PRINTED IN THE UNITED STATES OF AMERICA

10   9   8   7   6   5   4   3   2   1

Cover design by Jennifer Heuer
Book design by Amanda Dewey

While the author has made every effort to provide accurate telephone numbers and Internet addresses at the time of publication, neither the author nor the publisher is responsible for errors, or for changes that occur after publication. Further, the publisher does not have any control over and does not assume any responsibility for author or third-party websites or their content.

*Penguin is committed to publishing works of quality and integrity.
In that spirit, we are proud to offer this book to our readers;
however, the story, the experiences and the words
are the author's alone.*

For Mamita, my parents,
and the generations that persevered

No, no, go not to Lethe.

John Keats,

"Ode on Melancholy"

Contents

The Forgetting River

ONE

Ancient Voices

Arcos de la Frontera, Spain, 2008

Rise. Pray. Hide. Flee. Feast. The bells of Santa María thundered commands across the pueblo of Arcos de la Frontera, one beat at the quarter, two at the half, and then a flurry on the hour.

The cast bronze choir of thirteen bells dictated orders in silvery tones, hum notes, and the rattle of a clapper that sounded only on Good Friday. They tolled for escaped prisoners and the agony of the dying. They celebrated saints' days and weddings, prayed for pregnant women in labor, and mourned, with delicate chimes, children in tiny coffins.

And the notes of the bells lingered for more than six centuries through the uneven maze of a white pueblo that gripped a three-hundred-foot sandstone ridge. It was an ancient border town on the *frontera*, the frontier deep in the south of Spain that once separated warring kingdoms of Muslims and Christians.

The church bells were the pulse of all who lived along the steep lanes of Arcos, with a throne on the ridge that gave the pueblo a haughty air of power and grandeur.

Now Arcos struggled to pay the bills for the lights that illuminated its fiestas. But it boasted a Goya painting in its seventeenth-century town hall. And it still claimed a royal title bestowed by Philip V in 1706: "The noble, very loyal, faithful, and monumental village of Arcos de la Frontera." During the medieval era it was rich enough to afford seven churches, two of them fiercely competitive basilicas. Santa María and San Pedro vied for their flocks with the voices of more than two dozen bells. Their notes ushered in the morning as I walked toward Santa María's neoclassical belfry, which loomed over the yellow cliffs and the green Guadalete River.

It was possible to escape the sunny plaza at the peak by three winding lanes. Below a white arch, a narrow passage of gray cobblestones plunged away from the precipice. But I couldn't shake the dread that something was taking place around me. Something I couldn't understand. Something I couldn't flee. One thing was clear: True deliverance in Arcos de la Frontera comes in one of two ways—the church or the river.

The grimmest task for the bells was to toll the melancholy processions of the pueblo's unwanted exiles through the *casco antiguo*, the town's center and historic quarter.

When secretly practicing Jews in the 1600s were discovered and banished from the pueblo's plunging cliffs, the mournful notes enveloped them as they marched along a cobblestone chute with no exits called Inquisition Lane. It led from a whitewashed Inquisition jail with a single barred window north to Cerro de la Horca, Gallows Hill. The site of the local gallows was reserved for the worst punishments for *bandidos* and murderers, whose corpses were quartered and scattered, medieval justice that carried punishment beyond the gallows. Later the name of the lane was changed, erased like most memories of the Catholic Church's "Holy Inquisition Against Depraved Heresy." The crusade, tied with a Spanish royal edict to expel Jews in 1492, was not officially revoked until nearly five hundred years later.

What were the secrets that the bells could confess from those times? I found the notes arresting. They taunted me at times, goading me onward, to my present folly: hunting family ghosts.

I had settled here among the bleached houses of Arcos to find some broken spiritual shards of myself and my ancestors. We were Catholics, but I suspected we were actually Sephardic Jews whose identity was stolen, hidden, and lost for centuries like a missing key. Or at least the clues pointed me in that direction because I had doubts. Doubt was my religion.

It was why I had traveled thousands of miles over the

years from Paris to San Francisco to the Guadalete River, a jade ribbon against the craggy rock of Arcos de la Frontera. Guadalete was named for the waters of the Greek underworld in Hades, where ghosts of the dead sipped from the river Lethe to erase earthly memories in order to be reincarnated.

I had come here to dredge memories of the forgetting river, searching for information on a totally quixotic quest. I wanted to feel the sparks of old souls. It was why I had spent months poring over pages of graceful old Spanish handwriting on worm-eaten Inquisition records and leather-bound histories of Arcos that can be found only in private libraries. It was why I had picked up and moved in the searing heat of summer to a white house balanced precariously on the ridge, or Peña Vieja—Old Rock—for its battered and lined face.

Odd as it seemed, it was the reason I was trying to strike a conversation with the bells.

Every quest has a romantic origin. Mine started with the call of the bells of Santa María that regulated the life of this pueblo. The oldest, which had chimed hourly since 1437, was forged by a Jewish bell maker who centuries ago left a mysterious message.

In turn, the message was eternally ignored. Generations of families along the labyrinth of Arcos were drilled in the curt commands of bells of bronze, copper, and tin, but few people knew anything about the bell founder, as the craftsman was called. Some mourned that the bells themselves were losing some of their ancient fluency—the complex voices in the strokes, the strike notes that identify individual bells, the deep hum notes that linger and leave shivers.

"Over time, the bell ringing has become more basic," said Antonio Murciano, one of the town's many Renaissance men with an eclectic résumé: aging poet, retired lawyer, the pueblo's regular concert announcer, and expert in something totally Spanish, flamencology—flamenco studies. The bells were his neighbors for all his life, and they marked his childhood and defined his poetry. I sought him out in his enormous library, stocked with dozens of titles by Señor Murciano and his brother. Since the 1950s, he had nurtured a cottage industry of fellow poets that had given the pueblo the nickname "Arcos de los Poetas." Their torrent of words filled books and local libraries, including titles by the pueblo's longtime mayor.

"How many summers, how many winters, have we listened to the hours sounded by the bell ringers," he read aloud one of his poems to me. *"From below the bell tower, my memories are the chimes of the glory and the soul, of birth and fire."*

His criticism that the current art of bell ringing has become more plainspoken struck me as rather severe. Since I first started visiting the pueblo in 2003, Santa María had resolutely protected its traditions, resisting automated bells that had spread throughout Spain and to its enduring rival, San Pedro.

The first signs of this stubbornness were wet sheets flapping in the hot gusts of the *solano* winds from a balcony of

Santa María's belfry. The laundry belonged to Santa María's live-in bell ringers, two seasoned *campaneros* who were the last to live in a bell tower in Andalusia. Their apartment lay below an enormous, grinding eighteenth-century clock. They rang the bells daily, with special performances for the August 5 feast of the town's patron saint, La Señora de las Nieves, the Lady of the Snows, whose fifteenth-century image was enshrined in gold in the cathedral. According to local legend, the image appeared in a snow-fed mountain stream after being hidden during the Arab domination of Arcos, until the pueblo was reconquered in 1264 by Christians.

From friends who lived below the belfry within waving distance of the *campaneros*, I learned that the bell ringers boasted distinguished pedigrees. There was an old Spanish saying that the *campanero* is born, not made: *"El campanero nace, no se hace."* So it was with Manuel and Dolores, a married couple with chimes in their blood and thick, knotty ropes dangling outside their second-floor flat within the cathedral of Santa María.

Dolores is a dark, solidly built woman with short clipped hair, who favors vivid print dresses. She gave birth to her three children in Santa María's bell tower, and she wheezed mightily when she climbed to the tower's landing by their apartment. That is where we met for the first time, high up in the bell tower after I buzzed at the ground floor and asked her husband, who was baffled and polite, if I could visit the belfry. Manuel invited me up to the landing, where I waited for his wife.

My first impression of Dolores was the slow thud of footsteps. From the open window at the landing, I heard the chatter of Spanish and the relentless pounding of a hammer. And then she emerged from a stone staircase, her face weary, dark brown eyes shadowed by deep hollows. She was startled when she saw me, but recovered, assessing me as *una turista*. A rare tourist on a pilgrimage to her ancient belfry.

My Spanish has a nasal American accent. I fumbled for plausible reasons for invading her very private preserve. I came here to Andalusia for my own personal right of return— to recapture what might be a homeland, to salvage beginnings and an identity that my family forgot. I was trying to reclaim a region where centuries ago my ancestors fled from the port of Cádiz and then scattered in all directions— to Cuba, to Costa Rica, to Colombia, and then ultimately to California.

Along the way, family history had been discarded and rewritten, relatives buried with memories of where we came from, information about why we left and who we were tossed aside. I was pursuing a story that should be felt as much as told. I was less a tourist than a sojourner.

The brazen notes of Santa María's bells were deeply familiar. But I could summon only a few faltering sentences to explain my mission to Dolores.

"Señora, this may sound very odd. But I feel like the bells are talking to me. What are they saying?"

She nodded without questioning, gazing at me with a quizzical expression.

"Perdona," I stuttered, "I mean something other than twelve o'clock."

The bells, I knew, were more than just a signal of time passing. They were also a voice of advice and warning, of longing and despair. The notes carried toward the groves that surrounded the town, and dominated all feeble human noise.

Dolores dropped stiffly into a high-backed wooden chair, sighing that bell ringing is a heavy responsibility. From her expression, she clearly thought I was a strange foreigner.

The cathedral had done little to boast about its dynasty of taciturn *campaneros*. They were not mentioned in any guide offered by the local tourist office next door to Santa María. The last recording of a bell concert from the church, circa 1982, was a collector's item, and on the landing within the church is a dusty glass showcase with fading photographs of Santa María's bells swathed in yellow paper, ignored and overlooked.

Dolores and Manuel preferred to let their bells speak. They cut off conversations. They marked siestas, summoning children to bed for prayer. In previous generations, the bell ringers delivered surprisingly complicated messages to mark a death: the age, the sex, the social class. The warning bell toll—*toque de alzar y ocultar*—is a series of sonorous tolls and menacing pauses and then a flurry of frantic, silvery notes, a direct order. Rise. Hide.

The oldest bell in Arcos de La Frontera is named La de las Horas. That would translate to something like "On the Hours." It was an ancient bell of huge dimensions and fine walls that hit the lower octave with a lingering hum. Since 1437, it had marked the passage of time, known by its fond nickname of La Nona, Grandmother.

I tried to ask Manuel about La Nona's bell maker. But instead of answering, he turned away to tug the ropes of the bells for the noon hour, mingling the rich voice of the sixteenth-century bell, La de los Cuartos, with the higher tones of La de las Horas.

Most of the time, when Dolores and Manuel spoke, they picked their words cautiously, with the care of climbing the steep tower where a simple cross of hardwood commemorates two men hanged from the tower in the nineteenth century by French invaders. Dolores was particularly mysterious when I asked her about a bell combination from the Inquisition, a special toll for the procession of prisoners. She looked toward Manuel for a distraction.

"*Menos golpes,*" she snapped, ordering him to reduce the strength of his rope tugging. From the church balcony, the early morning sun blazed over the valley and the Guadalete River. The *solano* winds, blowing from the southeast—from the African desert—swirled through the Plaza del Cabildo, a historic site of Inquisition trials. I studied her impassive expression, waiting for an answer.

"We don't talk about those things."

I nodded. My Spanish was too limited to press again for an answer with a slightly different twist in my questions, my stock tool as a journalist. I already knew a lot from my research. Each bell had its own distinctive voice, particularly

La Nona, which had always intrigued local town historians. Unlike other bells, it didn't have a religious name for a saint. Instead a Latin message is inscribed in Gothic lettering on the thick edge of the cup of the bell, with some words misspelled.

D. ANTÓN LÓPEZ ME FIZO

MENRTEN SANCTAM SPONTANEAM

HONOREM DEO PATI ET LIBERACIONEM

I found no reference to this in Santa María's official church history, but there was a nineteenth-century book in the local Arcos library with black-and-white illustrations. Stamped on both sides of La Nona, I learned, was a coat of arms of the castle of León, suggesting the bell might have been a royal gift.

The bell maker's declaration was clear enough: "D. Antón López Made Me." One vital clue, historians say, was the bell maker's use of the initial D. before his name, which stood for "Don." It was a fifteenth-century title, according to the town's nineteenth-century historian, who wrote that the honorific was never used by craftsmen in Andalusia at the time unless they were Jews.

Don López had forged another mighty bell that hung in the bell tower of the cathedral of Seville with his name and a similar message. But what did it mean? It appeared to be a crown.

Sanctam means "sacred"; *pati*, "suffer"; and *deo*, "God." *Menrten* was a misspelling, but the intended Latin appeared to be *mentem*, or "mind." Could *liberacionem* mean "freedom"? Had he left a message of God, suffering, and freedom?

><·<

In Arcos, the art of bell ringing passed down through four centuries of the Barrios family to Manuel, a slight, leathery man in his sixties with a manner as severe as a church gargoyle. When he tolled the bells, though, he softened, a smile tugging at his lips as he pulled the heavy cords. He was born in this bell tower, learning the ropes like the five generations before him.

His late mother, Concha, "La Campanera," started ringing the bells at ten years of age and continued into her nineties, receiving a framed papal commendation. It was a grueling job that could last a whole day for the election of a new pope. "You have to know the rhythms and the pauses," Concha once said when she was in her eighties. "Any error is like listening to a flat note from a virtuoso opera singer."

Manuel's father was nicknamed "El Cani," or "Dogtooth," which naturally I assumed meant something ugly, as was confirmed by some of the town's residents. He learned to play with his family at the rival church of San Pedro before marrying Concha and moving up the summit of Plaza del Cabildo to live with her. Manuel's grandfather was also a master bell ringer, whose coffin was lowered from the bell tower of San Pedro when he died. According to local legend, he brought a newborn donkey into San Pedro's tower apartment till it grew so big that the family was forced to make a painful choice: Who would live in the bell tower?

"Where is the donkey?" he was asked.

"What could we do?" he replied. "We ate it."

By most accounts, El Cani was a chain-smoking story-teller who loved to talk about his bells. His squat looks drew obvious literary comparisons. "The French had their legend of Notre Dame, Quasimodo, created by Victor Hugo," a local historian wrote in a glowing obituary in 1969. "We had the same figure, but a real one of blood and bones. El Gran Canino, 'El Cani.'" Unlike his garrulous father, Manuel carried on the legacy with a grim sense of duty. He confessed no favorites among his bells. *"Todos son iguales."* All are equal.

I asked to climb to the top of the belfry to see La Nona for myself. At such a request, Manuel and Dolores looked alarmed. They made it clear that outsiders were forbidden to be that high up in the tower because it was too dangerous.

Their response startled me; I wasn't really sure how to go forward. I made a few more awkward attempts at conversation in the small vestibule by the dangling ropes. A few steps down the landing of the belfry, I could glimpse inside their cozy cathedral apartment. I knew they were eager to go home, but too polite to turn me away to return to their duties.

So I bade them good-bye, picking my way carefully down the dark staircase into the hard white light of afternoon. As I wandered outside through the pueblo's cramped alleys, the morning sun cast shadows across bleached seven-hundred-year-old houses and arches, a melodrama of light and shadows, detours and dead ends. I passed orange trees drooping with fruit, and wandered streets that tapered to dead ends the size of small rooms.

Then I heard a rustling movement, and crazy laughter drifting on the wind. I froze. Blood rushed to my head and I was haunted by the thought of ghosts tugging at my sleeves. I peered through an ornate sandstone arch, but I saw no one. The only sound was La Nona. One beat, a pause, another chime, pause. Tolling for every hurried inhabitant.

How strange it was that the living and dead phantoms could ramble along streets, chained to history. I kept walking, pondering the message of the bell maker. God. Country. Freedom.

La Nona, I thought, was owned by the church of Santa María. But after centuries of tolling, the voice still belonged to its master, D. Antón López.

TWO

Living on the Brink

Arcos de la Frontera, 2008

We settled into a former medieval bordello on the cliffs of Arcos, along a hill that dropped toward the crumbling stone Tower of Treachery. The pueblo's last surviving gate, it stood guard over the eastern side of Old Rock, which was twisted to form almost an amphitheater. From the second-story windows of the apartment I shared with my husband, Omer, and daughter, Claire, we could see a donkey and a lone white farmhouse, surrounded by alfalfa and bordered by the Guadalete River. The river flowed, cool and swift, starting in the Sierra de Grazalema at an elevation of thirty-three hundred feet and conquering Andalusia at its own pace for one hundred miles before curling into the sparkling blue Bay of Cádiz.

There Christopher Columbus set sail in 1502 on his fourth and last voyage for the Americas, perhaps with one of my ancestors aboard.

Like the Guadalete, a quality of willful forgetting flowed through the pueblo, where people had a habit of losing the meaning of all symbols and history that surrounded them. It was a trait—or perhaps a skill—that my family and ancestors also shared. I hoped that I did not.

I referred to the old bordello in Arcos as our house, not quite comfortable with the word "home." Some writers move to foreign lands to chronicle the restoration of a house in Tuscany or the transformation of vineyards in Burgundy. Some chronicle the charm of growing up in the old Jewish quarter of the Marais in Paris or the hapless fate of settling into a two-hundred-year-old farmhouse in the Luberon Mountains in Provence and dealing with butchers, grocers, and truffle hunters. I came to Arcos to restore something less concrete: a discarded identity.

When I grew up, ancestors, ancient relatives, and the past were not part of my sense of family. Something of my family's exile from assorted countries had rubbed off on me and affected the way I think. I always felt like an outsider—this sense of not being deeply connected to all the branches and roots of my family and always observing from a distance. So I concocted a classic literary plot and cast myself as the protagonist. A stranger arrives in an exotic town to dig in the archaeological site of memory. Start with the territory. The adventure follows.

For me, the allure of this pueblo is the *frontera*, the hazy frontier that Arcos occupied in the clouds between the reality of today and the history of the town with its mystery and air of tragedy. "One foot in the sky, one foot in the frontier" was the philosophy scribbled on a chalkboard on the sidewalk outside a boutique hotel on Calle de la Corredera, whose owners—including a former business journalist from Madrid—had transformed themselves into innkeepers. The citizens of Arcos have long been border dwellers, with their sights on two worlds, their day jobs and sidelines as poets and performers.

Could Arcos have this life-altering effect on others? Could I reclaim our abandoned past like rebuilding some crumbling house?

I passed into this alternate *frontera* when I strolled past a pure white home with a secret passageway dug clear through to the other side of the cliffs. Heavy double doors of scarred oak and iron opened to a swirl of inlaid yellow bones and curved bits of spinal columns—a legacy of the Gothic side of Arcos de la Frontera, where the living and the dead coexisted on a daily basis.

I sensed the parallel world at the square of the summit of Plaza del Cabildo, which faced the brink of the gold and green Spanish plains, where medieval bullfights and royal weddings were staged over the centuries. Every now and then the valley tempted tortured souls to simply fly off the rock like the pueblo's *golondrinas*, the swallows that rise and fall as if they were trying to erase the sky with their wings.

At the Plaza Boticas, blazing with sunshine against bright blue sky, people sipped dark *cafés solos* on a placid outdoor terrace below the scarred wall of an old jail. Long ago, in the seventeenth and eighteenth centuries, the body parts of executed prisoners hung in an iron cage until the remains were picked clean by wind and insects, as a public warning about the severity of local justice.

The most haunting lane was Calle de la Cuna—Cradle Street—which was the city's forgotten Jewish corner. It plunged so steeply that iron handrails were bolted to the walls of houses. At the foot of the alley were an old granary— whitewashed like the other houses—and other silent buildings that were a legacy of the old quarter. A money-changing house. A shop for Hebrew arts.

The names of Jews who lived here in the pueblo have vanished, except for traces of the ancestors of Isaac Cardoso, a prominent philosopher and physician who was forced to convert to Christianity and fled the Inquisition in the mid-1600s to live in Verona, Italy. It was Cardoso who wrote that the medieval illness of "melancholia" was a uniquely Jewish disease because of the wounds of sadness left by forced conversions and exile.

In another little white house lived Andrés Velásquez, a doctor and likely converso who was the author of the definitive sixteenth-century *Book of Melancholia*, which explored the origins of what was a medieval border disease of displaced people.

I gripped the iron against one white wall coated thick with lime like whipped cream. There was nothing to mark the name of the melancholy place, not a street sign or an azulejo ceramic tile to remember what surely is its old Jewish soul. The rest of the *casco antiguo* was marked along its twists and turns with ubiquitous blue-and-white ceramic tiles quoting poets about the city's beauty. "Arcos de la Frontera—symbol of Andalusia, graceful architecture, and the values of the south."

Calle de la Cuna, though, did not merit an azulejo. It was as if God had made the spirits here pay for the beauty of the lane by taking everything. The people of this Jewish quarter had died twice: once when they were banished, imprisoned, or punished, and again when they were forgotten. Forgetting is the injustice. My senses sharpened. I knew the old white houses were observing me. Past and present is an illusion. Places, like people, keep their scars and footprints.

Maybe I was drawn here for something more prosaic. People could actually pronounce my name. For decades I had been forced to painstakingly spell and pronounce it, from American grade school classes through French job interviews—C-A-R-V-A-J-A-L with a hushed *h* for the *j*. Here nobody asked. When I heard the Andalusian accent, it reminded me of the Spanish spoken by my father and grandmother from their native Costa Rica, where Spaniards from the south settled and stamped the tiny Central American nation with their speaking style.

The Andalusian accent reflects the blast of summer heat that in August can rise to 110 degrees. In the morning, the sun slithers up the ridge, climbing to the top and becoming an oven at the summit of the pueblo. Words, syllables, and energy are conserved in the hot afternoons. Consonants are dropped, endings chopped, and naps are taken, leading to jokes among northerners in Madrid that Andalusians are so lazy they can't be bothered to finish their words. Goofy Spanish cartoon characters speak like southerners. Spanish actor Antonio Banderas, of Málaga, kept his own southern accent for the voice of Puss in Boots in the Shrek animated film series, but switches to standard Castilian for more serious roles, as in a Pedro Almodóvar movie. Unlike him, though, I am stuck with the telltale evidence of my nasal American accent when I speak Spanish.

From my rooftop terrace, above the street, I kept watch over a steep, curving lane of rust-colored tile roofs and thick white walls. Arcos is part of a chain of more than nineteen white mountain villages that cling to the Sierra de Grazalema. One of those pueblos is called Algar, a bleached refuge founded as Santa María de Guadalupe de Algar by an elderly aristocrat, Domínguez López de Carvajal, the viscount of Carrión and marquis of Atalaya Bermeja. I didn't know if he was an ancestor, but I felt drawn to this wanderer who returned to Spain from Mexico sometime in the 1730s after a vision. He feared he was going to die in a violent storm battering his boat between Mexico and Spain. While en route he saw a glowing Virgin of Guadalupe, the national saint of Mexico and patron to Indians and Jews who were forced to convert to Christianity. The legend was, he pledged that if he survived, he would found a village in the most remote spot in the Sierra de Cádiz and dedicate it to her. It took him almost forty years; he established the town in 1773.

Arcos de la Frontera is the gateway for these pearls of white villages. Its population totals thirty thousand, including those people who live in the enclave of newly constructed houses on the outskirts that are not part of the ancient center of the pueblo. The old quarter, with its labyrinth of Moorish arches and white houses, has fewer than five thousand people. For those inhabitants, Arcos is a seductive place that has a way of transforming lawyers into poets, bakers into singers, and some flamenco performers, unfortunately, into part-time drug dealers.

I didn't know any of this when I made my way to Arcos for the first time. I discovered the pueblo in the most unglamorous way: while browsing in a tourist office in nearby Jerez de la Frontera, where I was staying. It is the biggest city nearby and is a haven for sherry wineries about twenty-one miles to the west of Arcos. British tourists tend to flock to Jerez on direct discount flights from London for the sherry tours and the spectacle of the Spanish kings' powerful white Andalusian horses that train daily in historic stables draped with pink bougainvillea vines. Other tourists bring strappy black shoes with strong court heels for cultural immersion in a thriving industry of flamenco schools.

I belonged in the latter category, having signed up for a weeklong dance package in the beginner's class at the Centro de Baile Jerez with a red-haired British guide named Amber, who acted as a counselor for all the beginner dancers, introducing them to the teachers. On the battered wooden dance floor, I stood in the very last row beside a shy computer programmer and a group of Scottish librarians who yearned to tap their inner fire. Behind them in the second line of dancers were a lithe Japanese office girl and Lola, a London transvestite with shiny black hair and short, flouncy skirts, who had already stoked the flames.

I didn't feel the passion myself for flamenco dancing—I lasted long enough to master a few basic steps—but I could see something in my daughter, Claire, then six, who from the sidelines mimicked the teacher with much more emotion and fire than I did. At one point in the lesson the flamenco teacher commanded, "Hold your head high like you are swallowing something bitter."

My daughter stiffened her spine, narrowed her eyes, and arched her fingers into a sharp weapon, like she was attacking memories. Even at that age, she seemed to feel something profound. Could it be a spark of the past? I wondered.

When the classes finally ended, I gratefully reached for a tourist map, vanishing into the countryside—without a tap of my flamenco heels—with my family in tow. Narrow backcountry roads led us from Jerez de la Frontera toward Arcos, about eighteen miles northeast.

We traveled under cloudless blue skies and coursing winds, past fields of alfalfa, prickly pear cactus, and scorched sunflowers with brown and bowed heads. My ambition for the side trip was to indulge in a Spanish voyage that would be equal parts vacation and search for family history. I knew that my family on my father's side must have left Spain in the province of Cádiz to get to Costa Rica. My parents had not told me much about my ancestry as I was growing up, probably because they didn't have much information to share.

Since my life was always a constant state of movement, trading states and countries, I was certain that this restlessness was something ingrained from generations of ancestors who abandoned birth countries in search of refuge and possibility.

Then September 11 happened, the bright blue Tuesday of my canceled good-bye party at a trendy Chelsea restaurant in New York to celebrate my departure for Europe and a new job. I moved across the Atlantic a few days later, untethered by memories of that day, the mushroom cloud in the north tower as my 8:43 train from Long Island approached Manhattan, the haunting images of people choosing to jump from the top floors of the burning World Trade Center rather than face death in the intense heat and flames. I carried with me my daughter's childish drawing of that day, planes in flames, my head on fire.

Only later did I realize how profoundly it had affected me

and intensified a strange yearning for something indefinable—
a sense of refuge, of belonging. It was what they call in Spanish a feeling of *añoranza*, a longing for home, to be whole.
This longing held sway over my life choices and became part
of my existence. Before moving to Europe, I had lived on
both coasts of the United States, worked at seven newspapers
as a journalist, and shuffled through Los Angeles, St. Petersburg, Florida, and Philadelphia. I then spent seven years in
New York writing for *The New York Times*, and then moved to
Germany and ultimately to Paris, where I settled into a job at
the *International Herald Tribune* and *The New York Times*. My
French husband and I had moved into a honey-colored stone
farmhouse in green country along the river Oise, which once
drew fabled painters like Vincent van Gogh, eighteen miles
northwest of Paris.

In contrast, most of my friends from my suburban Northern California high school stayed faithful to our roots and
quirky Bay Area conventions. They bought houses in rings of
new developments around our wealthy suburb of San Francisco. Our homecoming queen married a strapping star foot-
ball quarterback. My junior prom date, a swimmer on the
boys' high school team, fell in love with another man. Count-
less times I returned to California, but I always left, yearning
for something else, something indefinable, something besides
the bracing smell of eucalyptus trees and the brilliant blue
skies. Everyone adores San Francisco, but I grew up taking
the city for granted, wondering why it was a prize trip on
game shows and knowing I couldn't stay.

Perhaps it was because I came from a family that believed in fresh starts and good luck. Or perhaps it was because I was searching for a sense of belonging. Our name, Carvajal—or one spelling version of it—means "lost place."

When I arrived in Arcos, I was carrying a green book that my father had sent me with information about eleven generations of his family that ultimately traced back to Spain. But the chapters ended without an explanation of why they had left.

I wanted more—more than what I read. I wanted to explore the beginning of my family, to fill in the deep, black holes of family memory. My inspiration was my grandmother's ring, a thick gold love knot, coppery pink, which represented all the mysteries of my family and was stamped with a hallmark that dated back to the early 1800s. My Costa Rican grandmother, Angela Chacón, had worn the ring as long as I could remember. As a young girl, I had watched my dark-eyed, vivacious *mamita* remove it carefully before plunging her hands into a foaming sink of slippery dishes. My older cousin, Rosemary, used to beg to slip the ring on her finger, but Mamita—as we called her—refused to relent, characteristic stubbornness that propelled her through life.

I never wondered why she wore the band. Then one day it lay cold in my hand—ready, finally, to pass on to Rosemary—while I got Mamita's man-made pearls from a rare trip she took to the Spanish island of Mallorca.

Twisting the band in my fingers after Mamita's death at eighty-four, I pondered how to unravel our past. Had I always been so selfish, presuming her life began only when mine did? I realized I didn't know my grandmother at all. It was only after she died that I learned the ring's meaning. But the family's past was like piecing together an ancient Egyptian message from pottery shards. My clues were black-and-white photographs of my grandmother in a filmy veil and a wedding dress, with a wan, childish smile. Her expression masked the pain of a marriage arranged swiftly by family and friends after the death of her father, mother, and aunt when my grandmother was only seventeen. Her father, Julio, was an accountant who traveled through Central America, and the family story was that he died of tuberculosis contracted in the tropics. Mamita's mother and aunt died in their forties within hours of each other, both from heart attacks, too late, according to the death certificates, for Catholic rites.

Years after Mamita's death, I used to stumble upon her old perfume bottle, pushed back into a dark corner of my night-stand in my French farmhouse. Many times I tried to throw out the stale, golden Anaïs Anaïs to avoid the sharp scent of loss. But the perfume made me think of everything about her, memories of the musical jingle of her gold charm bracelet, engraved with the names of all of her nine grandchildren. And the charms reminded me of the sugary, golden *cajeta* candy wrapped in waxed paper that she brought every time she returned from Costa Rica. Today it tastes to me like childhood. Most of all, when I breathed Mamita's old fragrance, I smelled the heady scent of stubbornness.

Mamita had abandoned Costa Rica sometime in the late

1940s, also discarding her husband, José Francisco, a prosperous dentist who found solace in other women before and after
her departure when ultimately they divorced. She settled
in Mexico City for a few months and then moved back to
Costa Rica after her Mexican apartment was burglarized. In
1947, however, Mamita pressed on in a plane that made a
stormy landing in El Paso before continuing on to San Francisco, where other relatives were waiting. She had money and
prime real estate, up to seven houses in the center of San José,
Costa Rica, according to family lore, but she lost much of her
small fortune when she paid off José's gambling debts. Yet
she kept her golden ring and her fierce stubbornness when
she landed in San Francisco with her two teenage children:
my father, Arnoldo, and his older sister, Eugenia.

Many years later Mamita would mention a lover, the
director of a medical laboratory named Manuel, who, in a
desperate handwritten note delivered to her by a courier, had
urged her not to leave Costa Rica. They had laid plans to
move together to San Francisco, but when he couldn't obtain
a visa because of his past Communist Party affiliation, she left.
His note warned her that she wouldn't survive in the United
States because she could never master English. She told me
later that she ripped the letter into little pieces and sent them
back in the same crisp white envelope he'd sent. She also
shredded his photos, a habit that she applied with the same
zest to her wedding pictures, trimming away the halves with
my grandfather's narrow, aristocratic face and light cat-blue
eyes that inspired his nickname, El Gato. Only after she

died did I learn that Manuel had given her the ring for her engagement, which she wore without any explanation all her life. It was then I finally realized how human she was—that she had dreams, feelings and scars. How did I miss what was so clearly there?

On the surface, her gutsy story seemed to be a classic immigrant's tale of clawing up the rungs of the American ladder, of studying English and toiling in a San Francisco toy factory, stitching frilly dresses for Nancy Ann Storybook dolls before landing a job at Bank of America. Yet among generations of relatives, we counted royalty, Latin American politicians, ambassadors, and presidential advisors. And the bond we held in common was an overwhelming, restless yearning to roam.

After Mamita's death, we searched through the belongings she had brought to my parents' suburban house on her final visit before she suffered a stroke. Inside her wallet was a little motivational poem that brimmed with the birthday card optimism of a wanderer:

Follow your dream.

If you stumble, don't stop and lose sight of your goal.

Press on to the top.

For only on top can we see the whole view.

Can we see what we've done and what we can do.

Can we then have the vision to seek something new.

Press on and follow your dream.

Mamita's story—and the larger tale of our family—was not about what we knew. It was a tale of an identity, a culture, and a religion that was lost. We had pressed toward the top, but our past and where we came from were still a mystery, still unknown, still something that our ancestors had chosen to hide long ago and guarded so carefully that they failed to pass it down to us, to me.

Certainly, it would be a relief to cross off my list of lost objects the Bermuda Triangle, Atlantis, home, identity. After I visited Arcos a number of times, the pueblo simmered in my mind through day jobs and daily life, a lingering fantasy that by returning to live high on its yellow cliffs I could confront the past and reclaim an identity.

We all dream of going on a great journey, but then the years pass and still we have not sailed. I had a sense of longing, something unfulfilled. For that reason I was drawn to the timeless rock of Arcos: mysterious, unknowable, apart, and utterly haunted by what humans left behind, good and evil.

THREE

First Impressions

Arcos de la Frontera, 2008

The first time I entered the ancient doors of our new Spanish retreat on Calle de Callejas, the bells were tolling.

We had made forays between France and Spain many times before I decided to settle in Arcos de la Frontera for a summer to test the endurance of my romance with this village. Still, I was wary.

The façade of the seven-hundred-year-old house we rented was a sheer white wall standing three stories high, with a window at street level caged in black wrought iron. Calle de Callejas was so narrow that when the municipal minibus passed by and I was just outside the front door, I flattened myself against the house wall to leave a few inches of space for the driver to negotiate between both sides of the street. One morning, I watched a municipal bus driver scrape within inches of his friends with a sunny smile, joking, "I am going to kill you!"

Our upper flat, with its open courtyard, rooftop terrace, and tiled brick floors, is typical construction of that period, with a discreet courtyard at the entrance that masked signs of wealth in the home. The upper flat and the empty lower apartment had been totally remodeled, repainted, scrubbed, and installed with gleaming appliances. Our living room and bedroom windows looked down on weather-beaten tile roofs and the Guadalete valley below. But within the courtyard, there is still an ancient catch drain efficiently designed centuries ago. It was fashioned to capture rainwater in a cistern for a *pozo*, a small well with a bucket that had vanished in the makeover.

The neighbor who provided the key to our rental house was Stuart, a British expatriate who lived down the hill in a house that doubled as a bed-and-breakfast and loomed over the cliff precipice. His working uniform was paint-stained jeans, and he introduced himself with the assumption that I was yet another newcomer hypnotized by Arcos.

It had happened to him, a charter member of a class of new arrivals made up mostly of British expatriates who settled in the historic old quarter of whitewashed houses, dazzled by the *frontera*. Unlike their Spanish neighbors they had cash—bank accounts rich with British pounds soaring against the euro and the profitable sales of London homes to pad their accounts further. They poured their money into the old houses and set themselves up as hoteliers, changing sheets, serving tea, and mastering Spanish.

"In the old quarter, everybody knows everything and sees everything and knows what day you arrived and where you're going," Jim, a British teacher turned bed-and-breakfast owner, declared to the local newspaper. He described falling in love with Arcos on his first visit in the early 1990s, charmed by its simple pleasures: the fragrance of blossoming orange trees that line the main streets, the splash of water fountains, the pueblo's mysterious tragic air.

The English were not the only new immigrants. The cloistered, thirteenth-century nuns' order of the Mercedarias Descalzas also started absorbing immigrants to participate in prayer and vespers. To the convent in the old quarter began streaming young sisters from a satellite order in Kenya. They quickly mastered the convent's tradition of baking and selling honey-almond cookies and golden *madalenas*, fragrant muffins that tasted sweet on the tongue.

The culmination of the expatriate invasion was the brief arrival of a Dutch television reality show production team with bulky television cameras and fuzzy boom microphones that seemed utterly out of place on the town's cobblestone streets. The film crew moved into the historic center, taking over one of the ancient white houses to create a competition of visiting Dutch couples for a show called *De Spansoons*, "Dream House." Couples were vying for a chance to remodel and win their own bed-and-breakfast, Casa El Sueño, the House of Dreams. The competition was won by a young Dutch and Belgian couple, whose website shows a beaming family portrait on a windswept beach with their three children. When I walked by the house, I could glimpse, past the wrought-iron bars, a spacious breakfast room and a long, spare wooden table. All of the four-story, four-hundred-year-old house had been redone, some of the work completed during the competition among Dutch couples vying to be innkeepers. That included a popularity contest among local inhabitants who dropped their ballots into a wooden barrel. The winning family built picture windows overlooking the valley, something no Spanish architect would have condoned because of the brutal afternoon sun in that direction. They kept the original antique doors in the white house, a nod to a previous inhabitant, Cristóbal, a barber who for the past forty-five years had presided over his cramped barbershop footsteps down the hill. While giving my husband a ten-euro haircut, he laid down his busy scissors to search for an envelope of black-and-white photographs of the old house with the very same wooden doors. One day, he said, he hoped to share them with the Dutch innkeepers. It was clear the new residents had not mingled with the old.

So far Casa El Sueño had proved a dream for the Dutch family, partly because they were able to attract a steady stream of tourists from their home country who were captivated by the show. But for Spanish innkeepers, relying on local tourism, an ongoing economic crisis in Spain has wreaked hardship. The pueblo's residents call it La Crisis, like some monster that lives in their midst. When a real estate boom in construction—fed by low interest rates and a surge in immigration—imploded in 2008, the result was that many people lost their jobs in the deepest recession in Spain in fifty years. Middle-class families were hit hard, especially in Andalusia, where unemployment rates soared to almost thirty percent. Jobs vanished for eighty percent of the men in the pueblo who worked on construction jobs and also battered hotel and bed-and-breakfast owners who lost Spanish customers who scrimped by eliminating vacations. Cookie-cutter housing developments, started in the boom, lay empty and unfinished on the outskirts of Arcos.

Marriages and relationships were often casualties of chasing shattered dreams. While we were in France, our rental apartment sometimes doubled as a temporary refuge for husbands or girlfriends who were in the midst of ruptures. In one case, we heard about a double split: an expatriate who divorced his wife in another country for a younger Spanish wife to create his dream of a rural bed-and-breakfast. Then she left him for a local man.

The house where I lived in Arcos was a real estate investment roiled by economic forces. It was purchased at a low price by a Spaniard and then sold to a British and American couple who paid far more to gut and carefully restore it. The house was for sale, like dozens of others in the old quarter. As the homes were bought by outsiders to modernize, there was a real danger that the pueblo's old quarter could lose evocative memories.

In some white villages in Andalusia, the arrival of the British expatriates initially drove up prices, with local residents elated to sell their homes to move to more modern houses located on the edges of the pueblo. The locals fled parking shortages on the hills and creaky plumbing while newcomers were left to deal with the joys and challenges of living in the romantic old quarter. Eventually, some of the British expatriates started to realize that with the economic recession and the collapse in the value of the pound, the Spanish sun could not pay their bills.

Our British neighbor, Stuart, had traded a career as a computer programmer for the more romantic life of a hotelier. When we arrived in Arcos, he had custody of the key to our house, and so he offered us a brief introduction to the new neighborhood. He escorted us to our new retreat and as he showed us around the house, my husband and daughter broke away to survey the rooms and sunbaked rooftop terrace overlooking the valley while I stayed with him.

Stuart talked nonstop—a reflection, perhaps, of his solitary life. I tried to pay attention to him, but from the minute we stepped into the house I felt a current trembling on my skin, pulsing out of my fingertips. Sometimes the body recognizes things before the mind catches on.

I tried to focus again on Stuart's detailed litany of his latest home improvement projects, when suddenly I heard faint childish shrieks. Footsteps thundered down a red iron spiral staircase that connected the rooftop terrace to the upper flat. Stuart ignored them, continuing to talk until my husband, Omer, rushed toward me and cut him off.

"Don't go up to the roof!" he said, nursing his right hand.

"What happened?"

"Wild bees are everywhere. They attacked from five nests."

Behind him, Claire wailed.

"It's burning. It's burning, Mama!" she said, rubbing her upper arm, red with two spreading welts.

Undisturbed, Stuart wished us good luck and made a hasty exit. My husband and I looked at each other in panic, vowing to stay away from the rooftop terrace until we talked to some Spaniards who could give us advice about coping with bees. I cautiously climbed up the red spiral staircase toward the rooftop and saw a few lingering scouts of bees, circling in the air, with long segmented legs that I never had seen on the fuzzy bumblebees of my youth.

It was an inauspicious introduction to our ancient house; I didn't even know the word in Spanish for "bee sting." I discovered later it was *picadura*—vital information when you're seeking an antidote at the local pharmacy.

That night, once Claire and Omer were asleep, my dreams began.

I was standing in a circle of hazy faces whose terrified voices rose from whispers to a fierce hum of bees, a mixture of fury and fear. We were debating whether to run, but as in most of my dreams we were frozen, unable to face or flee the menace. Suddenly, long-haired men in tunics surrounded us. Clenched in their fists were stout wooden clubs. Their eyes glistened and I heard screams of pain. Then darkness. Then the tolling of bells.

I woke with a dry, achy throat, pushed off the covers, and then checked Claire's makeshift bed on a bright orange fold-out sofa in the living room. I leaned closer and could hear her breathing deeply. She was also dreaming, twisting her legs between the sheets. I pulled the blanket over her shoulders and waited for her to wake. It wasn't long before she opened her eyes, saw me, and rose from her stupor. She sat with me at the kitchen table to drink orange juice and eat one of the golden muffins made by the cloistered nuns.

"Somebody punched me in the stomach," Claire told me sleepily. "Then I woke up."

No amount of gentle coaxing could elicit more details, but we both shared the same unease in the house that was making an aggressive introduction.

Claire's dream summed up my own anxieties. Perhaps we didn't belong here. Looking around the spare living room of thick white walls and tile floor, I felt the force of the house and heaviness in the air. Maybe it was trying to communicate something to our family—people who had never lived here before, but whose ancestors may have walked or run along these streets. Later, when I got to know our neighbors, people would talk to me about the distinct personalities of their houses as if there were a simple frontier between the living and the spirits of the dead.

A British hotel owner, for instance, promoted the "powerful energy" emitting from her spacious inner patio with vaulted ceilings as one of the desirable features of her five-hundred-year-old house. Across the street from us was the battered and locked door to an apartment where inexplicably no one had lived since the previous occupant had been found dead years earlier.

Like all families sharing the same house, occasional clashes between worlds erupted. The fiercest dispute ostensibly involved La Casa de Muñecas, the Doll House. It was a short walk from our flat and I had passed the house along Calle de Jesús Nazareno many times while on my way toward the summit of the Plaza del Cabildo. Nearby was a *mirador*, or viewing point, for San Agustín, a sixteenth-century church marked with the Jerusalem crosses of ancient crusaders—and the frantic object of a local fund-raising campaign because it was in danger of collapse with the humidity gnawing away its foundations.

The bolted wooden door of the Doll House, set deep inside white walls, was always closed. It was topped by a blue-and-white ceramic tile with the number 12 and a tiny crusader's cross. Four years before we settled here a family of five started raising complaints that surfaced in the local newspaper, *Arcos Información*, with the headline: "A Stable Family Suffers the Presence of Spirits in the House." The mother, according to the article, revealed their strife because she was fed up with an unruly spirit—a little blond boy, about nine years old and dressed in old-fashioned overalls and a plaid shirt. Life with a youthful spirit was not pleasant.

According to the family, they suffered punches, pinches, slaps to the head, and shoves down a narrow stairway. A teenage daughter insisted that a doll hanging on one of the walls moved her eyes and hands and pleaded: "Don't hurt me." They felt waves of cold and heat in the house that intensified after a neighbor broke through a connecting wall that led below to a cave. As proof, they offered medical records listing their injuries and invited paranormal investigators into their home.

After a year of complaining—which also led to intense neighborhood debates and years of considerable television coverage in Seville—the family in the Doll House was finally moved to new housing by the pueblo, which owned the house. Some neighbors were sympathetic, confirming that spirits were a presence in another house on the street. Others told investigators that the haunted house was a ruse that helped an impoverished family obtain a better house for their children, who suffered from asthma and health problems. But no one was secure enough in that belief to remodel and move back into the house.

A fake complaint or not, the tale played on deeply held superstitions in Andalusia. Strange noises and events are part of life in the pueblo, where dank caves constitute a subterranean universe. Secret passageways honeycomb the pueblo's ridges with tunnels leading directly to the sunny courtyards of houses along the ridge. The dark caves are linked to every primeval fear—ghost tales, local superstitions, buried skeletons—and influence the mystical culture of Arcos.

Legend has it that a dragon slumbers within the old rock, making noises along the bluffs when it rouses. On moonlit nights, another local superstition is that a Moorish woman wanders the ramparts of a fortress at Plaza del Cabildo. It is the spirit, according to the legend and local guidebooks, of a woman who was the favorite of one of the pueblo's ancient Moorish leaders, who was murdered at a macabre dinner in the eleventh century where all the guests were suffocated on orders of al-Mu'tamid, the poet king of Seville. When she learned of his death, the woman transformed into a vulture—yearning for vengeance.

Was some strange spirit stirring within my own family? When I shared my dreams with my husband, I was surprised at his response. He said he woke up from a nightmare of Nazis beating prostitutes.

"Maybe the old house is telling us something, but is also trying to get used to us," Omer said.

"But we never had a problem in France. I don't remember any chatter with our three-hundred-year-old farmhouse."

"Give it time. Maybe this house is so old it has feelings."

At night, when Arcos became a place of living memories, I felt the fear. I was afraid of whisperers, plunging cliffs, and strangers at the door. In the day's bright sunshine, our dreams vanished.

But a few days later, when we bought handmade honey

candles at a local ceramics store, Claire shrieked suddenly. She insisted she had been stung by a golden beeswax candle. I didn't believe her at first. But then I examined her hand and noticed a tiny prick of blood welling from her index finger.

I wondered whether it was another sign that we were unwelcome, after the bee attack on the rooftop terrace and the unsettling dreams. Then a wave of anxiety hit me as if I had been pricked. What were we doing here? I reminded myself again that I was here for a very simple reason: my identity.

The more I tried to figure out who we were, the more I wanted to confront the past. I wanted to dredge the truth about our origins. I wanted to live in the land of my ancestors, to feel their struggles that still lived within me. I wanted a conversation with the bells of Santa María, but maybe it was beginning with our pure white house.

FOUR

La Crisis

Arcos de la Frontera, 2008

The most sinister nightmare in the pueblo was not a ghost but La Crisis. The Spanish economy was sagging and some neighbors were struggling to pay their mortgages, for garbage service, even loaves of bread. From our roof terrace—which was now bee-free—I spotted glossy green potted marijuana plants, nourished in interior courtyards, for sale in the pueblo's underground economy.

As the economy contracted, beginning in 2008, the pueblo's main lifelines of construction and tourism shriveled. The local city hall struggled, canceling costly public events and delaying payment of debts. The town owed 6,000 euros to a neighboring police union in Bornos to officers who provided special security for a fiesta. It failed to pay a local business-man who continually implored officials to pay for his services installing twinkling colored lights and equipment for *ferias*. Other public institutions were closed: a covered pool, a day center for senior citizens, and a vintage 1910 theater with a marble plaque that marked the day it was restored and re-opened with great fanfare in 1993 by Queen Sofía of Spain.

When would the economic crisis end? It struck the pueblo like the plague—the Black Death—that lingered in the town for almost ten years during the mid–seventeenth century, with no cure except perhaps a miracle.

After I paid the water bill at a local municipal office, the clerk showed me a stack of overdue payment notices on her desk and then pointed to another box with more envelopes.

"I had my water turned off," a woman said matter-of-factly while we stood in line at the post office, with its heartbreak-ing view of the valley.

"Really?" I said.

"We're using well water. Works fine," she said, referring to ancient rainwater *pozos* in interior courtyards.

It was high summer, full of torpid afternoons, when the blistering sun was conquered only by air-conditioning or the slow sip of cold gazpacho soup topped with melting ice cubes. The sharp click of a hand-painted fan—an *abanico*—was a measure of the heat, with women reaching into their bags for a fan to flutter across their faces as they sought refuge in the shade.

During the summer it does not grow dark until almost

midnight and we were guided by the bells of Santa María, our sense of time transformed. We called noon morning and eight p.m. late afternoon; we strolled out for dinner at ten p.m. Local flamenco shows at restaurants were advertised to start at ten-thirty, but no one breathed a note till close to midnight, effectively driving away exasperated tourists from France and Germany who didn't realize it was an old custom to delay performances in order to increase the volume of drink and tapas orders.

I savored this life. I liked sitting during the long, blue summer nights in the outdoor terrace of Bar Hostal Zindicato, in a building that had been an outpost of Franco's dictatorship. I liked their two-euro tapas, shrimp brochettes wrapped in bacon, stuffed eggplant, and Iberian pork, served on little white plates. I liked to study the large families gathered around the tables, cluttered with *tubos* of golden Estrella Damm beer and little glasses filled with garlic broth and tiny *caracoles*—snails. I liked guessing how many generations had lived on the ridge of Arcos de la Frontera and how many more would remain. Such an exotic notion—staying in place.

It was the season when immigration patterns reversed and Spanish construction workers headed to France in search of jobs while their wives picked green grapes at the local vineyards, a taxing job in the relentless heat that was ordinarily ceded to desperate foreigners from Guatemala and Ecuador. A neighbor, María José, came to me in tears to borrow money for food. She was in her thirties, a tiny woman with three boys and the third generation in her family to live in Arcos. She has nine brothers and sisters, and both her husband, Juan, and her father have lost their jobs in the spreading crisis. Most of the men in Arcos prospered in the construction boom, Juan among them, taking a private minibus at four-thirty every morning, in the dark, to drive north to work on a construction site in Seville.

When María José came to me, she and Juan had been anxiously waiting for money owed to him by a Seville contractor who had disappeared behind locked doors and dodged the calls of desperate men pleading for payment. She told me she was too embarrassed to ask her parents for aid because they were also struggling; her father had been laid off by the local branch of the giant Carrefour grocery chain.

I gave her some money before we headed down the rock to buy her bags of rice, oil, tomatoes, and eggs. She came back later with a foil-covered ceramic bowl brimming with cold gazpacho. When her garden on the outskirts of the village bloomed into harvest, she brought us enormous red tomatoes and curls of green hot peppers. Somehow her family of five managed to live on unemployment benefits of about $600 a month.

The crisis was so deep that one day she again knocked on my door for aid. I gave her money, but guiltily wondered whether I was skeptical enough. Was this survivor's instinct? Was this genuine friendship? I didn't know whom to trust. I didn't tell my husband about her requests, certain that he would have a harsher view. Yet I knew that she was desperately trying to raise money, preparing to carpool with other women to pick grapes for harvest—jobs that Spaniards once shunned.

I was untouched by economic hardship in Spain, having my own savings in France. But I could not ignore what I saw around me, even though I was absorbed with my own search for information about my family.

In the midst of La Crisis, it was not exactly the right time to pepper people with questions about the ancient struggles in the pueblo during the Inquisition. It was a delicate topic that was not easily broached, because most people would like to forget about that side of the pueblo's past.

But I've always been drawn to mysteries. And there's something here that draws me to the tingling of what Virginia Woolf called "the strange human craving for the pleasure of feeling afraid."

Silence has long served as a survival tactic in Arcos and the south of Spain, where Andalusians have lived under brutal repression from dukes to dictators. It is a skill that has been passed along seamlessly through generations, much as in my own family. One summer I visited the stone ruins of a Dominican church in the southeast of Spain near Níjar, a village with an ingrained culture of secrecy.

The crumbling remains of the church stood miles off the main road on a dirt path. But a landmark sign noted that it was immortalized by Federico García Lorca in his play *Bodas de Sangre*. The work is based on a 1928 murder provoked by a country bride with an inheritance who fled with her true love—her first cousin—on the morning of her wedding to another man. The match had been arranged by the bride's sister and her husband, who was also the brother of the prospective groom and stood to gain by joining two farms. The outraged couple chased down the runaway pair a few miles from the church, killing the boyfriend with three shots and attempting to strangle the bride, who played dead to survive.

What intrigued me about the crime was that the murder became part of the literary history of Spain, but the bride's divided country family resolutely refused to speak candidly about the events for more than eighty years. The bride, Francisca Cañada Morales—who was portrayed as a heroine by García Lorca—continued to live among them and never married. She died in 1987 at the age of eighty-four, but in death the pueblo added another secret. She is buried in one of Níjar's nearby cemeteries under a false name.

⊃•⊂

I would like to think I'm an adventurer in Arcos de la Frontera, rooting for secrets. But the beginning of my quest took me to rather unglamorous locales—the public library, the municipal cemetery, the cathedrals, and the pueblo's gray, melancholy streets. I wanted to understand the hard experiences of people who hid in plain sight under the constant fear of treachery by neighbors—whispers, surveillance, suspicious glances, and a scent of betrayal in the air.

I slowly pieced together scraps of information about my own family, benefiting from the meticulous records of the

Office of the Holy See, which listed Sephardic Jews after the fifteenth century. On the list were last names sprinkled up and down the family tree on the side of my grandmother Mamita—Angela Chacón—and my grandfather José Carvajal. Some were names so ancient that I knew nothing about their past, like Rafael Mogeizmes Farjado, a lieutenant governor of Costa Rica who died in 1775.

I searched through *legajos*, or handwritten Inquisition files from the seventeenth century that explored the double life of Jewish conversos in Arcos. One converso lived a few blocks from us on the edge of the cliff. He was Pedro Acosta, a hat maker and linen merchant and the son of a prominent rabbi. He was charged with secretly practicing Judaism in 1691 after a neighbor noticed that he failed to doff his hat when he passed a religious image of Jesus.

Centuries later, along the winding alleys of our neighborhood, there was still no escape from watchful eyes. People knew we arrived the moment we rolled our suitcases up the hill. Conversations carried from rooftop to terrace. Secrets drifted along the pathway. We could detect what the neighbors were cooking for dinner from the smell of *albóndigas* stew, meatballs cooking in red sauce, or the hot oil of potatoes frying for a Spanish egg tortilla. We could hear our neighbors' fights, their fears, triumphs, and songs.

From my living room windows, I could see two brothers who lived next door to each other without exchanging a word for years. The outdoor terrace of the older brother, Juan, overlooked the rooftop of Jesús. So Juan could smell drifts of his brother's cigarette smoke and observe that his sister-in-law was hugely pregnant.

Juan's wife, María José, was close enough to splash errant drips from a baby pool on the rooftop onto her brother-in-law, who cursed when he felt water from above. The opening shot in the family's cold war had been surprisingly petty. Juan's baby boy tipped over a vase. Jesús cursed him. Then silence descended between their homes, with each brother unwilling to bend to ask forgiveness.

Next door to the brothers was a Colombian immigrant whom we saw pushing a stroller down the slope. One day he vanished amid neighborhood headlines that he had been arrested for threatening his ex-wife. We saw her later at Paco's corner market, a vital institution on the steep hill run for three generations by Paco and his father and grandfather. They had recently traded a calculator for a cash register and Paco was proud to pass out crisp receipts. I couldn't help noticing when I bought a slab of El Capitán cheese that the throat of the Colombian's ex-wife was marked with a grim necklace of bruises.

Down the street was the self-styled mayor of the lane, whom I have named Monseigneur. We knew he had boasted to one newcomer that he was in charge of this corner of the pueblo because of his swelling real estate portfolio of property. He kept fellow neighbors in line by calling burly tow-truck drivers to remove cars parked illegally in the lane. One night we trudged down the steep hill toward the old city gate of Matrera Abajo to discover that our rental car had vanished. We found a scrap of a ticket on the ground, the only clue that the police had towed away our car.

The next morning I questioned one of the neighbors, who stood bare-chested with his black poodle at his heels, gazing at the hypnotic view of the Guadalete River.

"What happened to my car last night? It wasn't next to the 'No Parking' sign."

"The neighbor," he said, nodding to a bleached two-story house leaning against his—the Monseigneur's house. "He did it to me, and his father used to do the same thing before him."

Mentally, I pictured myself knocking on the door of Monseigneur and confronting him for his pettiness. But I decided it would take too much energy, and I wanted to get along with my new neighbors. So I held my anger and paid the $75 ticket. But I could not help thinking about the pueblo's past. What happened if a neighbor you trusted and saw every day reported you to an executioner for something as petty as not tipping a hat?

High on the rock of Arcos de la Frontera, justice is a flexible force, and Monseigneur wields the power to snap the attention of local police, who routinely ignore other infractions, such as motorcycle riders sweeping by without helmets as they ferry bareheaded toddlers and dogs. I marveled at how many people could fit on a motorcycle—four is the record—and the variety of tasks that can be accomplished while riding one: cigarette smoking, mobile phone conversations, delicate licks of an ice cream cone. We heard the insistent roar as they curved down our lane and then a click as they shifted into neutral to conserve gas on the drive downward.

"There are no laws here in Arcos," Ana, a shopkeeper with three children who lives on the modern outskirts of the town, told me. "There are police, if you know them." Then she shrugged.

As the economic crisis gripped the pueblo, police started getting tougher. They cracked down with tickets, apparently, to raise municipal revenues, and riders started sporting helmets. The annoying buzz of motorcycles also started fading; people could no longer afford to buy gas.

Watching over the motorcycle parade were the denizens of our street. One keen set of eyes belonged to Antonio, a beefy, balding man whose summer outfits tended to sleeveless white undershirts. I'm not sure what else he wore, because I never saw him away from his second-floor window. He emerged there with the regularity of the bell chimes like an unofficial street watchman, resting his hands on the frame as he held vigil over a gentle curve of the lane.

One night as Antonio hovered at his window, I introduced myself, standing two stories below. He responded with a familiar Andalusian expression: *"Conocemos todos"*—We know all—he said with a simple wave of his hand.

As early as the fourteenth century, the most miserable inhabitants of the pueblo lived along our hill, far from the rich who claimed the summit closest to the church of Santa María at its peak. The grandest houses, with marble steps topped by carved coats of arms, were owned by wealthy families who presumed they were immune from plagues. They refused to whitewash their homes like more humble inhabitants who coated their houses as a form of protection against the spread of disease.

In Arcos de la Frontera, practically anything can be whitewashed—houses, tragedy, history. Traditionally, the homes in white villages are coated annually with *cal*, a thin paste of lime and water that reflects the searing Spanish sun. It also has an antiseptic quality—vital during the time of plagues—because it can kill bacteria with its mild alkalinity.

There was something, though, about the relentless heat that made the inhabitants of Arcos obsessive about the purifying color of white. People thought nothing of coating their houses twice a year. One day I watched in disbelief as a resident painted up his walls to coat brick-colored roof tiles in white.

Our neighborhood lies a short distance from a huge white arch at the entrance of the old quarter, Puerta de Matrera, where the last of the town's four towers, the Torre de la Traición, or Tower of Treachery, still stands. The towers were key to the defense of the city when it was ruled by Moors; the pueblo fell in 1255 when the Tower of Treachery was breached by Christian invaders. The gate was the back entrance for the pueblo's undesirables, Jews and Gypsies. Gypsies were expelled from Arcos in 1587—almost one hundred years after the Jews. They were given two days to leave under the threat of huge fines.

From the arch, the Virgen del Pilar gazes down the lane, her feet strewn with plastic camellias. In the fifteenth century, most of the white houses beyond the arch belonged to Jewish owners. But their houses were confiscated after 1492, the year of the expulsion edict for Jews across Spain and Arcos. The Jewish occupants of Arcos planned well for flight. One of the oldest houses near the tower on Calle de Matrera Abajo has a narrow subterranean passage with a secret trapdoor that crosses under Calle del Cardenal Spínola to a staircase leading out of the jagged rock of Arcos de la Frontera to the valley below. On the edge of the cliff there are other houses with tunnels, including an enormous cave that was used as a secret Jewish synagogue with a back exit out the rock.

Our little house also served another purpose in the sixteenth century, when the red-light districts of *mancebías públicas* were common throughout ancient Spain and our quarter was the poorest part of the village. The ruling aristocracy needed diversions for their young warriors who helped ward off enemy Moors. In our pueblo, the first dukes of Arcos de la Frontera controlled the red-light district, the cluster of houses watched over by the Antonios of that time—*madres* and *padres* of the *mancebías*—who made sure those entering were the right age, the requisite *"edad de amores."*

When the construction crew gutted our house, they told the landlord that the house on Callejas was built by Jews because of its location and the way it was constructed, although the landlord didn't have any more information than that. One night, when we were still getting to know our house, I drifted to sleep in the old bordello and dreamed.

I dreamed I was with a man and a woman who were anxiously studying the steep cliffs below and, in the distance, the cool, green Guadalete River. Dark little figures picked their way in the dawn down the plunging rock of Peña Vieja. Inside there was a flurry of panicky movement as we gathered bread and cheese and blankets. Suddenly, there was a pounding and the bark of voices at the door. Someone snuffed out a candle flame.

I woke up, feeling relieved that I had escaped the dream. Yet the anxiety stayed with me, which strangely pleased me. In some primeval way I was connecting to the past.

FIVE

The Quest

Jouy-le-Comte, France, 2003

A few months before I discovered Arcos—or even knew its name—I received two large envelopes that were crammed into the mailbox of my stone farmhouse in France.

For a day, I simply ignored the envelopes with their stamps in the bright red and blue of the Costa Rican national soccer team, not that sure that I wanted to learn the contents. The envelopes stayed unopened in a pile of bills, beckoning from a world that I was wary to enter. Now and then I would look at the envelopes, thinking it was time.

Days after they arrived, when I finally opened the first flimsy envelope, there was no high drama, just a plain explanation from my father's first cousin Cecilia Carvajal Valverde. "With respect to the question of the Carvajals," she wrote in Spanish, in her blocky printing, "it's always complicated, as usual, with our family."

Her mother, a tiny, silver-haired woman with the profound brown eyes of an owl, was the one who protected the secrets, and her name was Luz, which means "light." She was my great-aunt, dead in 1998 of a stroke. Naturally, I never bothered to ask Tía Luz about our family when we sat around a dining room table in San José, Costa Rica, eating traditional cuisine of *gallo pinto*, black beans mixed with rice and eggs.

"Mama was the one who knew and she used to say that our origins were from *sefarditas*," Cecilia wrote, using the Costa Rican name for Sephardic Jews.

I reacted to this shift in the kaleidoscope of the family history with some shock and relief. Maybe this could explain why I always had doubts. I refused to think about the rosaries recited, the bended genuflections, the scapulars worn close to the heart, and the papery taste of a Communion wafer for a religion that might not be ours.

There was so much about Catholicism that I loved, for better or worse, that it had become part of who I was. I might have distrusted the sometimes dark power and history of the Church, but I remained grateful to the efficient nuns of Notre Dame who taught me to read. And even as an adult I savored the smell of church incense and the comforting mustiness of the small twelfth-century chapel by our French farmhouse where Joan of Arc had left two small crucifixes as a token of her visit.

Cecilia offered little additional information, suggesting that I track down an elusive family tree prepared by my long-dead great-uncle Rodrigo. According to family lore, he moved to Puerto Rico and restyled himself as the Spanish marquis of Zamora through the family line of my paternal great-grandmother Albertina Pérez Mora. My aunt Ligia Carvajal, the youngest of my grandfather's children with his third wife in Costa Rica, remembered the snide jokes about the noble title. But she had no idea what happened to Uncle Rodrigo's family tree.

"I remember my daddy telling me about this family idiot, a cousin, who paid for a trip to Spain and spent months in libraries making a genealogical study of our family. He thought he would inherit the title. But Rodrigo was the big winner, spending all his life living as a noble, when it was actually my father who inherited the title because he was the oldest son. Come to think of it, that would mean your father has now inherited the title."

The marquis of Zamora. Rolls off the tongue. So I called my father, Arnoldo—though by his seventies he had abandoned the *o* and went by the name Arnold.

He could not remember any discussions about the family's religious origins or about a family title, even though he had become the gardener who tended the family tree, tirelessly compiling bound volumes of genealogical research for each of his six children. I then approached my aunt and god-mother, Eugenia—or Jeannie—who had made frequent trips between San Francisco and Costa Rica, and asked what she knew.

"Sorry," Aunt Jeannie told me during an annual family picnic in the fall in the Bay Area. "I don't know anything about that. You have to understand the times. It wasn't something anyone wanted to talk about."

This lack of knowledge—about whether we were descended from Jews dating back to the Inquisition—amounted to a gulf of forgetfulness.

After hitting that wall, I started ordering rare books that tracked the lesser-known history of the Central American nation of Costa Rica. It is a tiny tropical country squeezed between Nicaragua and Panama, with a peaceful population that survived for generations by simply forgetting. When an aging Christopher Columbus set sail from the Bay of Cádiz in 1502 on his fourth and last voyage toward Central America, he carried an unusual crew, fifty-two families of Jewish conversos forced to renounce their religion if they stayed in Spain. Adventure was not their ambition. The crew was bound for the New World to save their lives and distance themselves from the Spanish Church.

The Spaniards anchored off the eastern shores of Costa Rica on September 18, 1502, taking refuge near Limón on the Atlantic coast for seventeen days. They were the early vanguard of Sephardic Jews who fled Spain over the course of four centuries, scattering with the Spanish edict expelling all Jews who refused to convert. The conversos spread throughout the Mediterranean, wandering as far as the Balkans and the Ottoman Empire and to Sicily, Sardinia, the Azores, Madeira, the Canaries, Mexico, South America, and Central America. Typically they prospered as merchants, bankers, and international traders, and they sought to protect their secret religious traditions through endogamy, marriage with other trusted converso families.

Some settled on Costa Rica's Atlantic coast in Puerto Limón and were trailed by small farmers from Andalusia who helped shape the country's soft and clear-spoken Spanish accent. Many extended Costa Rican families can be traced back fifteen generations to a tiny nucleus of about a hundred Spanish conquistadors who immigrated there between 1561 and 1599. For that reason, scientists consider tiny Costa Rica—along with Iceland—a rare international resource to study genetic patterns and inherited illnesses like schizophrenia and bipolar disorders.

One of the key Spanish conquistadors was Juan Vásquez de Coronado, who in 1562 led a group of eighty Spanish soldiers to Costa Rica to become the first governor and the chief builder of the nation, a legacy that endured. His uncle, Francisco Vásquez de Coronado, was also an explorer, roaming through New Mexico and marrying a converso Jew, whose father was the public treasurer in the new colonies. Juan Vásquez de Coronado is one of the main patriarchs of the Costa Rican population; genealogical studies show that his descendants dominated the ruling class for generations:

almost thirty heads of state and more than two hundred members of parliament.

Among the eighty soldiers who joined Juan Vásquez de Coronado was Antonio de Carvajal, whose wife, Ana, and daughter, Isabel, came with him. He would later become acting governor of Costa Rica after Vásquez de Coronado died in a shipwreck in 1565. Also in that same group of 114 conquistadores who colonized Costa Rica was Alonso Fajardo, an ancestor of my grandmother Mamita.

For Jewish exiles, the new territories were a refuge from the official bureaucracy of the Inquisition, which was presided over by two orders of priests, the Franciscans and the Dominicans, from hubs in Spain, Peru, and Mexico. After the discovery of Costa Rica, Spanish conquistador Diego de Artieda Chirinos recruited more than three hundred conversos from Spain to start new colonies. They set sail in two ships from Sanlúcar de Barrameda in 1575.

That legacy is often cited to explain Costa Rica's unique culture, from its nominal devotion to Catholicism compared with other countries in the region to one of its earlier national flags, a red six-pointed star that was flown between 1823 and 1824. Many local people had a cool relationship with the Church at that time. During the eighteenth century, the inhabitants of Costa Rica were punished by the presiding bishop of Nicaragua. The bishop excommunicated the entire population with its high percentage of Spaniards who indulged in the mysterious habit of settling far from the scrutiny of local churches.

The ire resulted from the fact that many of the Costa Rican inhabitants were converso Jews who resolutely avoided the Catholic Church. It was a custom followed by my grandfather, El Gato, who never attended church, scorned priests, and shunned the services even when my father made his First Communion as a boy.

Today some prominent national Costa Rican politicians and their wives are descended from Jews, among them former president Luis Alberto Monge, whose niece Giselle Monge-Urpí wrote a book about this history called *Descalzos en Palmares: Los Cripto Judíos en Costa Rica* (Barefoot in Palmares: The Crypto-Jews in Costa Rica). It was a copy of that blue book that my cousin Cecilia sent me, along with her original letter explaining that we, too, were descended from Jews. It was information that I accepted, a letter I tied up in yellow ribbon and put in a drawer of an antique secretary desk to ponder later. Shifting religions was not something that could be done in a day.

I would look at the letter many more times, unfolding the thin, flimsy paper and creasing it again, and then carefully tying it up in ribbon, as if this ritual would somehow make this information part of me.

My cousin Cecilia's answer seemed so casual, a bare minimum of information. And later, when she came to France, I would pepper her with more questions, but always it seemed as if there was nothing much she could offer to convince me that this was definitely true. It wasn't enough for me to change my life. As usual, I had doubts.

An Israeli researcher and philosopher, Schulamith Chava Halevy, who studied families in Mexico and in the southwestern part of the United States, found that typically the descendants of Sephardic converso families passed on their secret history in a variety of discreet ways. Cecilia's manner fit somewhere in the category of "casual transmission," information passed out briefly with no emotion. In fact, the researcher cited many examples of families who used variations of the same language, *"Somos judíos"* or *"Somos sefarditas"*—"We are Jews."

Most typically, according to Halevy, one relative from a younger generation would start raising questions and was usually referred to an elderly aunt who was the keeper of the family history and genealogy. Generally, elder women carried on the oral traditions because they were most conservative and less involved in organized groups that could notice their activities.

The curious were expected to divine the truth partly by themselves, or by piecing together, as in a puzzle, the meaning of family rituals and customs.

"Are we Jewish?" the researcher quoted a young man from the Southwest who confronted his father. The father replied, "Don't ask. Think."

And this was the riddle of the answer that Cecilia gave me when she sent the blue book. It was a slim history of Costa Rican "crypto-Jews," a term for people who practiced their religion in secret. In Hebrew they are known as B'nai Anousim, the forced ones. In a back section of the blue book

Cecilia sent me was a list of dozens of Costa Rican *sefardita* families, including my own, Carvajal. I pored over the others, counting nine last names in our family tree, including the maiden name of my grandmother, Chacón; her grandmother Solis; my father's grandmother Pérez; and the last name of my cousin Cecilia, Valverde.

✂

I searched my memory for forgotten clues until I remembered a telephone call I had received years earlier from a Florida freelance writer who had hunted me down through my newspaper byline. She told me that she was writing a novel about the Carvajal family from Mexico. Any relation? she asked.

Flustered, I apologized and confessed I didn't know, but she generously offered information about the Carvajals in Mexico, which I wrote down and excavated years later when I embarked on my own search. The archives at the University of California at Berkeley, she told me, house a precious collection of records from Inquisition trials that took place in the Spanish territory of Mexico. The archives, she said, documented the secret Jewish lives of the Carvajal family.

It was strange—and seductive—that these old and crumbling leather-bound books were a forty-five-minute train ride from my childhood home in Lafayette, California. Berkeley was also my alma mater and I knew a spokeswoman for the university, Kathleen Maclay, an ex-colleague from my career as a young reporter at the *Contra Costa Times*, a suburban newspaper that covered the area east of San Francisco.

When I contacted her in 2006, Kathy offered to shepherd me to the archives, housed in temporary quarters while its permanent building was being earthquake-proofed. She introduced me to several curators who explained the recent history of the rare documents, which had surfaced at the California International Antiquarian Book Fair in Los Angeles in 1996 to a buzz of gossip among antiquarians. The Inquisition records spanned a period from 1593 to 1817, the end of the Spanish colonial period in Mexico.

All of the documents were available on microfilm, but so far the scholars who had studied the meticulous Inquisition records had apparently not produced any books. An aging professor of Mexican colonial history had visited the stacks regularly, but died before he published anything about them.

When book collectors informed the Bancroft Library about the rich trove, university officials swiftly recruited wealthy alumni who pooled money to buy the sixty-one volumes from Mexico. The volumes had all been preserved but were too fragile for even occasional use. When I asked the curators who had saved the Inquisition records for centuries, they had only sketchy details. I had heard that a Mexican family had guarded them for two centuries, but the antiquarian dealer who brokered the sale to the university refused to be questioned by me. Invaluable records about the Carvajal family, including a trove of letters and a memoir, mysteriously disappeared in 1932, according to scholars, and then resurfaced along with trial records in 1996.

The mystery lingered in my mind as a curator led me to a meeting room where an antique wooden printing press stood in a corner. Who preserved records for centuries, and why? I wondered. My own family protected their secrets so zealously that they lost them. Were these Carvajals relatives?

At a wide wooden table, the curator laid down two wedges of foam, gingerly unraveling a *legajo*, a leather bundle of yellowing, brittle paper wrapped in battered dark brown leather and tied with a thong. The room was quiet and I could hear my heels click against the floor. The *legajo* looked so fragile that I was afraid to turn its pages. Its edges had crumbled and the pages were mottled. Isabel Carvajal's name, handwritten with a sweeping loop of a *j*, dominated the first page. The rest of the bundle was scrawled with slanted rows of beautiful black calligraphy, punctuated by brown pinpoints left by burrowing bookworms. Between the lines were larger, ragged holes, a legacy of the iron gall ink of the time, made from a boiled paste of oak tree parasites and water. When the mixture was too strong, the ink seared through the pages.

Library officials regarded the records as "one of our greatest hits," according to Anthony Bliss, the Bancroft's curator of rare literary manuscripts.

The third generation in his family to tend ancient manuscripts, Bliss looked the part in his golden spectacles and corduroy jacket with leather elbow patches. "We've learned nothing and forgotten everything from the Inquisition," Bliss told me, admiring the pages of graceful Spanish script. "But we've got these records here and we'll keep them safe for centuries, ready always for someone to learn from them."

I touched the book lightly, turning the pages. I felt an electric sensation in my fingertips, feeling the ink of some dry and meticulous inquisitor who had faced Isabel Carvajal. Was he wearing a hood as he recorded the banal household evidence against her? Could she read his eyes through the slits of his mask?

The *legajos* were the record of *procesos*, or trials, for heresy and "Judaizing" that took place in Mexico City against Isabel Carvajal and her sister, Leonor. The documents sketched out the life of Isabel, a widowed seamstress and daughter of a prominent Spanish family that left Benavente on the Iberian Peninsula for the Spanish colonies in northern Mexico, then known as the New Kingdom of León, or Nuevo León, a huge land grant that spread through the southern parts of the United States and the Mexican state of Coahuila, with its chief city of Saltillo. The Spanish Crown gave the land grant to Isabel Carvajal's uncle Luis de Carvajal y de la Cueva in 1578. According to historians, more than fifty percent of the original 170 settlers had Jewish backgrounds.

Isabel and her family had fled Spain for the territories, as had thousands of other secret Jews who chose exile and hardship rather than conversion at the hands of the Inquisition. The royal government had sought to choke off this exodus to Spain's colonies by barring the emigration of conversos, but resourceful exiles circumvented the ban through connections and well-placed bribes.

The leather volumes in the Bancroft collection recounted the mundane lives of men and women whose banal habits aroused the attention of their neighbors, provoking accusations of heresy for secretly practicing Jewish rituals. The telltale evidence of Isabel's crimes was the use of clean bed linens and clothing on Friday evenings, signs to demonstrate their observance of the Sabbath. The inquisitors also took note of other rituals—fasting and dietary restrictions, the shunning of pork.

A separate library list logged other Inquisition mementos, such as a frayed rope used in 1597 by a man named Blas de Magallanes to hang himself in prison while awaiting trial for scorning the Virgin Mary.

Among the list of Inquisition violations were witchcraft and sexual practices: defrocked priests intimate with parishioners, homosexuals accused of sodomy, or husbands charged with bigamy. With the passage of time, some of the religious crimes seem almost comic, such as a man who simply turned himself in to authorities for defiling a statue of Saint Joseph.

My mind wandered from the page to the people with the stubbornness to preserve the leather *legajos* for two centuries. How did they guard these records for so many years? Why was it so important to them that the *legajos* were protected and passed down? And how did they get out of the Church's hands in the first place? Maybe the records were salvaged when the Inquisition was formally abolished in Mexico upon

Mexico's independence in 1821, when the last person imprisoned for "Judaizing" was freed.

I continued reading the tidy lines in the old-fashioned Spanish that chronicled the torture that happens when power is unstable, when a regime is weak. The Mexican Inquisition, which started in 1571, was designed to eliminate the remnants of Judaism in the Spanish colony. Some historians theorize that the Carvajals, including Luis de Carvajal, Isabel's uncle and a conquistador and diplomat, were destroyed in a conflict between two governors over the region of Zacatecas.

The *legajos* at the Bancroft Library focused on the trials of Isabel and Leonor, who were turned in to authorities by her own brother, Luis Rodríguez Carvajal, who was being tortured. Luis grew up in Spain without any idea that his ancestors were Jews. He learned his secret origins after his parents moved the family to Mexico, and he adopted the Jewish faith with a singular obsession after surviving a storm at sea.

He and his family continued to attend mass regularly, but they avoided gestures such as the sign of the cross. Their safety depended on tight secrecy and trust in relatives and friends. Children were not given religious training until much older for fear that they might slip and bring a family to the dangerous attention of inquisitors or prying neighbors.

Luis, a favorite of the governor, had an older brother, Gaspar, a Dominican priest and an explorer. His church position reflected a common habit among conversos to send one son into the priesthood to gain access to Bibles that were unavailable to most people. But despite Luis's position and privileged connections, friends would one day betray him to the Inquisition authorities, and under torture he would betray his family. Luis and most of his immediate relatives, including his mother and sisters, were imprisoned by Inquisition authorities in secret cells in Mexico City. Although separated from one another, they managed to share messages smuggled in hollowed-out pears, an activity condoned by jailers who encouraged clandestine conversations to gain more evidence against prisoners. They plucked the tiny notes for safekeeping, which later were added to the Inquisition records that are stored today in the Bancroft Library.

"This is the road to the glory of paradise," Luis encouraged his sisters from his cell in May 1595, "and there is no other."

The Carvajals well knew the dangers and suspicions that new conversos were frauds who continued to practice their old rituals in secret. Even worse, it was whispered that Jews poisoned wells and sought the blood of Christian children for their religious practices.

Modern historians who have studied Inquisition records calculate that between 1560 and 1700, more than forty-nine thousand trials took place in Spain and its colonies in Mexico and Peru, targeting Jews, Muslims, and Christians accused of heresy. Punishment took many forms: family wealth and belongings could be seized, and accused heretics were isolated in solitary confinement in jail. The tedious legal process could be scheduled quickly or start years after someone was arrested. It depended entirely on the whim of the accusers. It didn't matter, as prisoners were forced to pay the trial and prison expenses. Neighbors were a source of betrayal and so were cellmates, who spied in order to incriminate others and perhaps mitigate their own punishments. And if authorities suspected that the prisoner was concealing anything, they resorted to torture.

Inquisition techniques during that era were not much different from reported abuses in, say, the American base in Guantánamo Bay, Cuba. Inquisitors did not consider torture punishment, but rather an interviewing tool. Today's waterboarding—or "alternative set of procedures," as former president George W. Bush once termed it—is nothing more than *tortura del agua*: simulated drowning. This was a basic Spanish tactic where victims were forced to choke on streams of water poured from a pitcher, with a cloth rag stuffed in their mouths to create sensations of drowning. The *garrucha*, or strappado, was another common strategy: suspects were suspended from the ceiling by a pulley with weights dragging down the ankles, which were connected to a series of lifts and drops. Other tools were the Judas Cradle—the victim was lowered toward a pointed pyramid aimed at his or her private parts—or the rack, used to extract "confessions" without respect to gender or age, including children. It was a tool to exact information that was referred to in Spanish as being "put to the question."

Typically at the Inquisition tribunals there were three judges. One was the *procurador fiscal*, who evaluated the accusations and questioned witnesses. Another was the *calificador*, who determined whether suspects had violated the religious faith. And the third was a court attendant. There were also three secretaries, including the *notario de secuestros*, whose duty it was to tally the wealth of the accused, which, when he was found guilty—and he almost always was—could be seized by inquisitors. These duties were paramount because the Inquisition tribunal lacked a formal budget and it depended on the confiscation of property and goods for its financing. As a result, many of the Inquisition's targets were rich men.

When the work was finished, inquisitors recorded the results: *"Confessionem esse veram, non factam vi tormentorum."* The confession was true and not coerced by torture.

La Familia Carvajal, a 1944 book by a Mexican author, Alfonso Toro, offered a chilling illustrated glimpse of the torture. It showed friars and men masked in peaked hoods surrounding the accused. In one illustration, Isabel Carvajal stretches on the *potro*, or rack, her head violently thrown back. In another, a woman lies on a pallet surrounded by robed men in hoods as one of them pours water down her throat. Early waterboarding.

After Luis Carvajal was formally sentenced to torture on February 6, 1596, he faced a blunt warning from the inquisitors. "If he die or be maimed of blood or mutilation of limb, let the burden be upon him and not us." When Carvajal was put to the question, he was escorted to the *potro*. It was a simple wooden frame, raised up from the ground, with rollers at both ends and ropes controlling the mechanism. He was stripped naked and tied to the rack with his feet fastened to one roller, wrists tied to another. As the interrogation intensified, he was urged to betray family and friends who were practicing Jews. When he resisted, a handle and ratchet tightened, stretching his body to increase the tension and pain until the cartilage and ligaments snapped. As the rack ground through its horrifying work, joints popped and dislocated, which released a rank smell of fear—a smoky burning odor. The naked, spread-eagled victim, vulnerable to hot irons or pincers, was a brutal warning displayed to others who sometimes confessed to secret Jewish rituals merely at the sight of a victim with swollen wrists and ankles bloodied from the bite of the ropes.

With the grinding pulls of the ropes, the pain became too great for Carvajal. He betrayed his sister, Catalina, as a "Judaizer." An inquisitorial notary recorded the facts, even counting the number of screams.

"Tell the truth!" Carvajal's inquisitor demanded.

"Ay, O Lord, may this help to counter my act of abominable transgressions. Pardon me, O Lord, pardon me, have mercy upon me."

The rope twisted again and Carvajal wailed, according to the notary's notes. Sobbing, he confessed that his youngest sister, Anica, observed the Law of Moses. There was a fifth turn of the rope and then a break. When Carvajal had time to recover, the rack rolled six more excruciating twists, stretching his joints. He blurted out more confessions about secret rituals of his mother and his sisters, his brother-in-law, and 116 other Judaizers in the town.

But in his pain, Carvajal was plotting escape. A few minutes after he was escorted outside the Inquisition chamber, he wrestled free of his guards and jumped to a courtyard one floor below. He was not seriously injured and was swiftly recaptured by guards, who appointed two prisoners they could trust to spy on Carvajal as he lay in prison.

In December 1596, his torture finally ended. At age thirty, after having named other practicing Jews, Carvajal was burned at the stake in a public execution called an auto-da-fé in Mexico City. His mother, Francisca, and four of their in-laws were also executed, along with three of his sisters, Leonor, Catalina, and Isabel, who were strangled first with an iron collar and then set on fire.

In the dry words of the detailed trial transcript that ultimately gave Carvajal a lasting legacy in history: "The body will be burnt to ashes until no memory of him remains."

SIX

The Enchantment of Fear

Arcos de la Frontera, 2004

Semana Santa, Holy Week, is the most perilous time in Arcos de la Frontera.

It is when the pueblo transforms from a drowsy village time into a siren and assassin. For a few reckless hours, massive black Lidia bulls roam free on Calle de la Corredera. A local ambulance stands guard to aid the injured, usually drunken tourists. The spring air, scented with incense and warm lilies, is the moment when romantics are most prone to fall in love with the pueblo's poetic lies. Easter week generates a kind of haze of enchantment when the whole town is caught up in the passions of music, religion, art, and spirituality and the giant images of Jesus and Mary weaving through the streets for hours into dawn.

For all those reasons, Semana Santa is the most important week of rituals in the pueblo—officially a national living historic landmark.

I remember when I was introduced to Arcos's somber religious rituals, which draw Spanish tourists from Madrid and Barcelona and muscular American soldiers from a military base in Rota. It was 2004, and the attraction was a week of sumptuous Easter processions through the winding streets, following rituals dating back to the sixteenth century.

On the morning of Holy Thursday, we struggled up the golden rock of the pueblo by car, negotiating tight lanes with the car's side mirrors pushed back to avoid scraping chalk-colored houses. Many of the white walls were scarred, residue of the constant scrapes of modern technology against seven centuries of history.

We came to a halt outside the Hotel Real de Veas, an ocher-colored nineteenth-century house with arched wrought-iron windows facing the town's main street, Calle de la Corredera. The Holy Week ceremonies are organized by ten religious brotherhoods, which historically were like guilds, made up of men and now also women who prepare months for this week with a rigid hierarchy of leaders.

Inside the hotel, the cool interior patio had glossy, deep-blue-and-white Andalusian ceramic tiles and potted palms. The lobby was presided over by the somber, bearded proprietor, Cristóbal. He greeted us and gazed back gravely with dark brown eyes the color of Spanish coffee.

"You're lucky. You arrived just in time for the singing of the *saetas*."

"*Saetas?*"

He continued patiently, ignoring my questions. "Tonight I have a special *saetero*, Pepe Alconchel, who will sing *saetas* from the hotel balcony. You should come if you have never heard this music."

Cristóbal patted my shoulder in encouragement and smiled again, as if sizing up whether precious information could be exposed. He left it to me to discover on my own the meaning of the music.

A *saeta* is more prayer than song, performed a cappella by lone singers to pay homage to eerily life-size wooden images of a bloodied Christ wearing a crown of thorns or a Virgin Mary shedding crystal tears. The ancient chant is performed while anonymous penitents in masks and enormous peaked hoods march in cadence along the cobblestones while holding burning white candles. Cristóbal assured me they bear no resemblance to the American Ku Klux Klan. But the clan clearly borrowed the images even though they are virulently anti-Catholic.

Saetas are chants pulled deep from the heart like tiny arrows. Federico García Lorca called the singers *archeros*. These archers save up raw emotions to perform once each year during Semana Santa, physically risking their voices because of the strain of singing without musical accompaniment, with deep, lingering notes from the impromptu stage of windy lanes and wrought-iron balconies.

"See if it speaks to you," Cristóbal encouraged me. He was an enigmatic man who gave occasional clues about his own past. He grew up in Arcos and drifted away to northern France, abandoning Spain during the long reign of the dictator, Francisco Franco. Many of the men in Arcos scattered to new countries during that period because they lived in the most impoverished and divided region of Spain. The Civil War is still a topic nobody likes to talk about in Arcos because bitter emotions remain deep on both sides of the political gulf that pitted Republicans against Franco's Nationalists.

Cristóbal and his wife, Mari Carmen, were eventually drawn home, investing their French francs in a mansion that they converted into a bed-and-breakfast that attracts tourists from across Spain and the occasional bicyclists from Germany. When Cristóbal looks out on the pueblo where he grew up, he sees streets where nothing has changed. He doesn't stray far, avoiding the eastern side of the ridge on Peña Vieja because he considers the neighborhood ordinary.

On this Holy Thursday, I noticed Cristóbal peering at the gray skies from the hotel's grand doorway.

"Where is the best spot to stand when the *saetas* begin?" I asked him in my halting Spanish.

"Tonight I'm not sure," he replied, studying the looming clouds. "I'm afraid it will rain." I knew that if it rained, the voice of the hotel's hired *saetero* would not echo along Calle de la Corredera for another year. Some of the town's ancient *cofradías*, or brotherhoods, would cancel their religious processions. The wet stones of the town's constricted streets were too slippery to navigate with baroque wooden statues that are traditionally carried in *pasos*, or floats, on the shoulders of *costaleros*, or "sack men." These brawny members of the brotherhoods who bear the floats are called thus because of the cushions that brace their necks. In the interests of historic preservation, the town's brotherhoods long ago eliminated a risky custom known as the Kiss because of the threat it posed to two treasured eighteenth-century wooden statues. It was the hushed moment on Easter Sunday when two brotherhoods paused in the Plaza de las Aguas with two giant pallets to press a rosy image of Our Lady of the Waters gently against a figure of a Christ child in a symbolic kiss.

That risky custom ended in the late 1970s, but today the wooden figures of the Virgin Mary and Christ still reign every Semana Santa over Arcos de la Frontera in various processions that can linger eight hours or more. The pallets on which the statues are carried still rock like boats of flickering candles above a crowd of onlookers, many of them believers, all of them eager to witness a procession that has been part of this town's history for hundreds of years. The pueblo's processions are intimate events compared with those of its urban neighbor, Seville, where more than fifty images of Mary are paraded through the streets during that city's Semana Santa. In Seville the grandest statue, La Macarena, a seventeenth-century carving, is escorted by a teeming entourage of more than two thousand penitents and men dressed as Roman soldiers.

Lumbering down the narrow streets of Arcos, the giant images were designed to wrench emotions. Centuries later, they still exuded power, with expressive faces of colored polychromatic wood, glass eyes, and soft wigs of human hair.

The richly jeweled virgins were dressed like medieval Spanish queens in lace and thick fabrics embroidered with silver thread and plaited with gold. During the sixteenth and seventeenth centuries, onlookers fell to their knees in prayer, weeping at the approach of the images. Today's spectators are more likely to shout *"¡Viva!"* and press their hands against the floats to seek blessings. But when the brotherhoods paused with swaying statues at the windows of the sick, women wept openly with the sorrowful Virgin for the hardship and pain they shared in crisis-stricken Andalusia.

The figures were hypnotic in a manner described by Antoine de Latour, a nineteenth-century French writer who was struck by the raw emotion that the carved statues evoked. "The crowd demonstrated a profound and sincere spiritual absorption, all profane thoughts fleeing from their minds, kneeling with their hands stretched out toward Christ. They had found the faith of olden times," he observed.

On my first Holy Thursday in Arcos, I felt a surge of emotion as the processions wove their way along Calle de la Corredera. I instinctively drew back from the anonymous penitents in the brotherhood, men who wore robes and coverings of an *antifaz*—a fabric that covers the face and shoulders—and enormous peaked cones. I studied the dark eyes of the penitents, which made me feel the pain of some primeval memory that I couldn't explain. Beside me, parents urged their children to move closer. "Look! The Virgin is weeping."

My husband was next to me and so was Claire, her hair tied in a brown ponytail and bleached by the sun. When I looked back to check on her, I was stunned to see my daughter—with so little religious training that she needed an introduction to the story of Adam and Eve and the forbidden fruit—fall to her knees. There was truth in the old Andalusian advice that if you don't believe in God, drop to your knees and pray. Faith will come.

I scooped her into my arms and whispered, "Look! Jesus." My emotional response to the procession was not much different from that of the legendary Spanish sculptor Juan Martínez Montañés—known as "the god of wood"—who was so overwhelmed to see his own works marching through the streets in the seventeenth century that he cried out in astonishment.

I comforted Claire, gently pulling her to her feet. I was a newcomer to these rituals, but when I felt the rhythm of the streets and inhaled its scents of incense and melting candles, I knew that I was an invader of what was mine.

I studied the masked men, overwhelmed with another blinding emotion: I wanted to rip away their hoods to see their eyes and the eyes of their ancestors.

SEVEN

A Faithful Andalusian

Arcos de la Frontera, 2004

Some say that a faithful Andalusian needs only three elements in life: a home, a burial tomb, and a brotherhood. No one seemed to embody those elements more than Manuel Pérez Regordán. His home was hidden on a sharp bend of a lane called Juan del Valle, named for a sixteenth-century Spanish writer who lived in the enormous white house. Every Semana Santa, all of the brotherhoods marched by Don Manuel's house and a doorway topped by three azulejo tiles, which marked his associations with prominent local clubs.

There was a fourth, shiny blue ceramic tile in the cool vestibule—"AQUÍ VIVE EL CRONISTA." Don Manuel was the town *cronista*, or historian. It was his job to probe and record the secrets of Arcos de la Frontera. His family had lived in the *casco antiguo* for more than nine generations, a family tree with branches that included a general from the Spanish-American War and an infamous bullfighter turned Spanish Robin Hood who sought refuge in the mountains and defied local authorities.

Don Manuel's enduring pride was his métier. His thick ivory business cards testified to his lofty position, embossed with a gold-and-red municipal seal and the title "Cronista Oficial de la Ciudad." There were several definitions but only one true description: village sage.

The first time I glimpsed Don Manuel was during my first Holy Week in Arcos. I already knew from the hotel owner, Cristóbal, that Don Manuel was the *cronista*, a position that charmed me. It lacked the connotations of some dry historian toiling away in isolation. He was something livelier than that, something more practical: a storyteller who chronicled the pueblo's quirky character from tolling bells to towed-away cars.

The *cronistas*, who work in most cities in Spain, are an intriguing breed of amateur historians with various degrees of training and often a propensity to promote their pueblos as more historically important than they are. But they are highly regarded and beloved in many towns.

Don Manuel looked like an accountant—which he was—a short man with thinning gray hair, spectacles, and amused eyes that were as unreadable as was his smile. He also worked as a banker and a teacher, but like so many others in Arcos, he led a dual life as a historian. Words were his way of ordering the chaos of life.

By habit, Don Manuel doled out his wisdom and stories from the dark wood bar of a tapas restaurant in the middle of town, below amulets of red chili peppers and cured sausages that dangled from the ceiling. Named Alcaraván, the restaurant was built hard against the rock cliffs. It was once part of an ancient jail that is still connected by a passageway to a privately owned Moorish fortress next to the church of Santa María. During the 1950s, Alcaraván was the literary heart of Arcos, with its seductive charms that tended to inspire industrious local residents to press more poems than bricks at the struggling local factory. Lately, the restaurant seemed to attract more tourists than poets.

Don Manuel, though, kept guard over Alcaraván's legacy as a literary redoubt. The cool cave of a bar was his longtime refuge, where he shared his stories. He liked to warm a glass of golden manzanilla, a fino sherry, in his hand, sip a taste of the dry southern plains, and then move on to another tale, another glass.

What animated the night was Don Manuel's appetite: for sizzling barbecued tapas; for a pale sherry with a taste of chamomile tea and a faint salty flavor of the sea. He lived to chase history—listening to idle talk in the plaza or reading ancient census counts of bakers, shoemakers, and lawyers. He created stories for the same reason that bees produce the region's golden alfalfa honey. It was an activity essential to what he was.

In any neighborhood of Arcos, residents know one another's business, but nothing beyond their own intimate blocks. As the town *cronista*, Don Manuel made it his official business to collect the history of all seventy-seven streets, lanes, bends, and crooks of Arcos de la Frontera. "Always he had a smile and some news of his investigations in Arcos," recalled one of his friends, who considered the pueblo lucky because Manuel qualified for a disability pension in 1999, freeing him to fill his days since then with the history of the town and its residents.

His friends were too polite to say it in their flowery tributes, but Don Manuel was also famed for his stubborn one-man battles and crusading fervor that reminded observers of Don Quixote. Within Don Manuel's own house, the walls were lined with hand-painted tiles of Don Quixote righting wrongs and thrashing evildoers. Every day he passed by a tile with Quixote's thundering challenge: "Coward! I demand to know what you are doing."

It was Don Manuel who fought off an attempt by the city in 1989 to rename ancient streets in the quarter for local poets, part of a broader plan to honor artists. But he directed his fiercest wrath at municipal officials when they hatched plans to destroy the remains of Calle de la Cuna's synagogue, whose history had practically vanished.

The duchess of Arcos, Doña Beatriz Pacheco, who herself was the granddaughter of a rabbi, transformed the synagogue into the Capilla de Misericordia, the Chapel of Mercy, in the 1490s. A woman who lived a life of contradictions, she demonstrated her Christian zeal to the pueblo by turning the synagogue into a refuge for abandoned children; she never had any children of her own.

After this transformation, the memories of the synagogue were lost, or perhaps more accurately, erased. Before Don Manuel, the nineteenth-century local *cronista* Miguel Manchego y Olivares simply ignored the Jewish quarter. The Inquisition in Arcos never happened, he wrote, because in "our city Jews, heretics, and Moors did not exist."

But Don Manuel knew better because of his own indefatigable digging in ancient archives of Inquisition records in Madrid and Cádiz. He was one of the rare observers in the pueblo who tried to read the messages of the scattered symbols in Arcos that were a legacy of the disappeared. Outraged at municipal plans to knock down the old synagogue for a housing development, he swung his sharp pen to shame local officials.

"In my hands I hold the town's proposal and I feel a mixture of surprise, stupor, and real pain," he thundered at the town's officials. "This will result in completely erasing what is left of the Jewish synagogue in Arcos. This is a street to remember those Jews, so persecuted in the history of humanity."

When I met Don Manuel for the first time, he seemed utterly mild-mannered to me—hardly a Don Quixote with a sword. Cristóbal had arranged an introduction at his hotel early in my first forays to Arcos de la Frontera. He mentioned casually that Don Manuel had a library in his house nearby and I pictured a room of dusty chaos. But when I was finally invited there, I marveled at a vast, orderly personal library so inviting that I wanted to sit down and burrow into a book.

The shelves were stocked with six thousand titles, a collection of almost sixty years that his wife, Mari, regularly dusted with odorless white powder to ward off mites. Many of the books he salvaged were from small cities that discarded them in the 1930s, during the Spanish Civil War. On one wall hung framed certificates and literary prizes, as well as a stern picture of a maternal ancestor, General Romero, who died a day before the explosion of the USS *Maine* in 1898, which provoked the war between Spain and the United States. On the opposite wall hung a letter from the Spanish royal palace, thanking Don Manuel for a book he gave Queen Sofía on her visit to Arcos in the 1990s. There was a cool marble table where he spread out his research in the center of the library.

Clearly Don Manuel had a craving to explain, to make sense of all those spirits floating along Arcos's streets like the phantom he remembers from his childhood. He claimed a ghost used to sit on the staircase of a house on Calle de Pesas del Reloj below the church belfry of Santa María. Neighbors whispered that he lingered because of a quarrel to settle with a living neighbor. When the phantom was in a gloomy mood, according to the *cronista*, he would roam the streets, dragging a heavy chain along the pavement—like a Spanish version of Jacob Marley. At one point, the ghost supposedly bumped into the mayor, Don José, sometime in the late 1990s, pausing briefly to temper his shrieks with a whispered "Good evening."

"There's no doubt that our ghosts are very well educated," insisted Don Manuel when recounting the tale in one of his histories. The author of more than thirty books, Don Manuel labored for years on his masterpiece, a self-published work of four volumes totaling four thousand pages called simply *The History of Arcos Through Its Streets.* The plain-vanilla books are packed with every obscure scrap of information from medieval tax payments and sixteenth-century occupations (eighteen tailors, two swordsmiths, and two fencing teachers) to memorable town murders and the complete course of the Guadalete River, starting at the source in the Sierra de Grazalema.

Over the decades Don Manuel walked the streets and probed their past—Dog Slope, Nun's Hill, Snow Lane, Bell Street, Notary Alley, Street of Chains. Each twist and turn had its own character. When Manuel stopped to listen, the streets talked to him.

His books, most of them self-published, are sold in unexpected places in town, such as art stores on Calle de la Corredera and at local hotels. Before I met him, I discovered Don Manuel's literary side at a ceramics store filled with glazed pitchers and cups and bowls. If I had been paying attention, I probably would have reached over his little stack of titles for a blue-and-white ceramic candlestick holder. But the vanilla-colored books gave me a flash of a persistent morning dream that had repeated itself like a video earlier that week.

In the dream I was reading aloud answers from a slim, ivory-colored book. Everything was calm and seemed perfectly reasonable. But when I woke up, I had absolutely no memory of what I was reading.

So I paused at the short stack of ivory books, all with golden titles that spelled out *La Real Justicia y el Santo Oficio de la Inquisición en Arcos de la Frontera*. It was a slim history of justice and the Spanish Inquisition in Arcos.

The text of the quirky book was written in green ink, chosen by Don Manuel because it was the signature color of the Inquisition. The cover was also marked with a crucifix, a sword, and a quill—a common Inquisition symbol that can still be found in churches and chapels in Spain. On the back cover, I saw a photo of a pale green star embedded in sandstone that startled me. I had never noticed the star before in Arcos. But Don Manuel had looked up high in the arches of the old synagogue transformed into a chapel. The green was the conquering mark of the Inquisition and the stars a legacy of the vanished Jewish quarter.

"They're here," I thought. "The ghosts of ancestors."

I purchased the book and read on, impressed with Don Manuel's research. He outlined the justice system that prevailed in Arcos during the Spanish Inquisition, which was a tribunal established in 1478 by King Ferdinand and Queen Isabella to ensure that Christian converts adhered to their faith and to stop Muslims and Jews from continuing to practice theirs. Though the tribunal was abolished in 1834, the Inquisition marked Arcos indelibly for all time.

Neighbors turned against neighbors, according to a short section in Don Manuel's book that listed some of the Inquisition investigations. The divisions were so fierce that the archbishop in Granada and religious authorities wrote to the mayor of Arcos in 1631 with a warning, scolding the pueblo because too many people had signed up as secular *familiares*. They were associates of the Inquisition who constituted a semi-secret police. Most of them came from two highborn families. And they had abused their authority, according to the letter, "causing scandal and gossip and giving rise to many clashes and tension that must be avoided."

For me, the most plaintive element of his book was a list of people reported to inquisitors by their suspicious neighbors. Nine witnesses turned against Antonia Josefa Montañéz, thirty-six, for practicing Judaism in 1758, four of them from the same family. Five neighbors reported Diego Alvarez, forty-nine, a single laborer. And the list went on.

As I read the pages, I started to toy with a crazy notion. Perhaps I could enlist Don Manuel to shepherd me on a search to unravel all the pueblo's mysteries and maybe, in the process, my own. What was the message of the bell La Nona? Why was the memory of Calle de la Cuna forgotten?

I was wary of approaching him directly about it, figuring that he needed to know me better before I proposed such an idea. My strategy was to test his reactions to sensitive subjects. When we met again at Cristóbal's hotel, Don Manuel brought along his wife, who was polite but largely deferred to her husband. Her presence made it even more awkward to broach what would surely seem an odd topic: Could he help lead me to the ghosts of my ancestors?

I started by asking Don Manuel a few questions about the meaning of the peaked hoods of the brotherhoods. Every time I saw them, they made me shiver with inexplicable emotions. But for him the hood was simply a uniform. He talked to me almost as if lecturing a new student.

"The hoods protect the privacy of the penitents," he said flatly, without explanation.

I suspected he was a little uncomfortable with this stranger. So I studied him carefully. Then I recognized a flash of my grandmother's familiar stubbornness in his eyes. I knew he didn't know me or trust me. But why should he? I was a foreigner—no matter what the past. And I recognized instantly that there was no way that he intended to speak freely. It was hard enough for me to connect to him in a second language, in Spanish. I was well aware that relationships evolve over time in Arcos de la Frontera, especially since some ties—and feuds—date back generations.

I desperately searched for a new subject with which to bond with Don Manuel. We had already discussed my work as a writer and my life in France and family in California and Costa Rica. It was too early to talk to him about converso Jews. His book about the Inquisition seemed like a safe topic. First I complimented his thorough research, which seemed to warm him. I watched his face soften a little, as if I had uttered a secret password.

"It is my most popular book," Don Manuel said with pride. "It sold out in its first two days." That meant he had sold five hundred books that he had self-published. Even in a town with amnesia about its history, there was a deep hunger for facts.

I was trying to come up with a general question that could lead to my plea for his help. So I just blurted out what came to my head.

"How long do you think I need to stay here to get a sense of Arcos?" I asked suddenly.

"Well, all your life."

"I don't have that kind of time."

He smiled back at me.

It was not yet time to seek a guide for ghosts.

EIGHT

An Unfaithful Catholic

Jouy-le-Comte, 2009

A framed black-and-white family photograph sits on my desk in the garret of my French farmhouse, a reminder of times when my sisters and I would dress up for Easter in white cotton gloves and silk flowers to visit my grandmother in the Castro district of San Francisco. We take photos not to remember, but so we can puzzle over them for the rest of our lives like exotic laboratory specimens. No one realized it when the picture was snapped, but in that photograph the future was obvious. How did I miss what was there?

On the back of the frame, in my mother's graceful

handwriting, is this: "1960, Easter Finery, San Francisco." My grandmother sits with my baby brother, Arnie, in her lap, surrounded by granddaughters in ruffled cotton dresses and straw hats, smiling from the porch of her two-story Victorian house. Mamita's large dark eyes avoid the camera. I am looking dreamily in the wrong direction.

During our Holy Week, we went to church on Good Friday, dressed up for Easter Sunday, and gathered at Mamita's house in San Francisco for family dinners. The Catholic Church was long a part of her weekly rituals and our own family traditions. Yet when Mamita died, her life was marked, at her request, in a private funeral home crowded with her friends and family: two children, nine grandchildren, and seventeen great-grandchildren. No funeral mass at Most Holy Redeemer in San Francisco, where I was baptized and my grandmother had long stopped saying her prayers. No stained-glass shards of light or organ music—just the unexpected music of my toddler indulging in a familiar chorus of the Barney the Dinosaur song, "We're a happy family."

At her memorial, we remembered the kaleidoscope of Mamita's life, the immigrant who had come alone to California with her two children and forged a new life even though she couldn't speak English. But there was so much about her that we—that I—had never probed. Why hadn't I asked her about the golden knot ring that she wore on her wedding finger every day? And why had she fallen away from the

Church when I was in my thirties, after making Sunday mass a warm weekly ritual of her life?

The last time I spoke to her on the telephone from New York, she had laughed about my then two-year-old daughter's mastery of a vital word, "cat." She conveyed a message of intimacy with her warm Spanish accent that she never lost despite decades in California. She was blind by then and in her eighties, but her stubbornness was fresh and youthful. Two days later, a stroke would run away with her mind, leaving me no chance to say good-bye or to realize I had questions to pursue. That would take years.

She didn't want a priest to preside at her funeral, and neither did my aunt Jeannie—Eugenia—who carried on the same tradition when she died of cancer in her Victorian house in San Francisco. Strangely, Aunt Jeannie accepted my gift of a rosary bracelet from the little white church of Nuestra Señora de los Remedios in Olivera, Spain, which she was wearing when she died. In last conversations with my father, she barred any priests from her bedside or her memorial.

We didn't ask. Some bitter clues were available easily enough from the headlines in the San Francisco newspapers. During the 1990s, nine former altar boys, including my cousin, now grown men, accused a powerful parish priest of molesting them on field trips to a lake outside San Francisco. The priest had dined in my aunt's house and performed the marriage ceremony of another cousin—I remember the wedding day as a swirl of white-and-emerald-satin bridesmaids' dresses. The San Francisco Archdiocese, which represents Catholics in San Francisco, San Mateo, and Marin counties, reached a $2.5 million settlement in 1996 with fifteen men molested as boys by the pastor and two other priests. But it was something we didn't discuss, especially my grandmother, who, after the family learned of the allegations and absorbed the priest's betrayal, maintained her thick and painful silence.

My own relationship to Catholicism also was marked by ambivalence. In the suburban ranch house on Padre Street in Lafayette, California, where I grew up, we were raised on rosaries and the Baltimore Catechism and Friday fish and Sunday sermons. That meant respect for priests and nuns and belief in a rather mysterious principle that I interpreted to mean that the Catholic families had to be numerous enough to fill a 1961 Nash station wagon. In our case, the tally was six: four sisters and two brothers. My parents were pious, their large brood of children a testament to Catholic doctrine banning artificial birth control.

I attended a Catholic elementary school where a portrait of Pope John XXIII hung next to a photo of John F. Kennedy, and I remember the moment when a scratchy unintelligible voice crackled over the school intercom to deliver the message that the handsome Catholic president had been assassinated. When we couldn't decipher the announcement, my second-grade teacher, Sister Mary Jean Therese, delivered the bleak news. I remember my mother later insisting to me as we watched the funeral carriage of horses carrying Kennedy's coffin on television that I was too young to understand the meaning of death. But I knew—death is as vivid as life in the Catholic Church.

When the priest demanded on Easter Sunday whether we believed Christ was born of the Virgin Mary and died for our sins, I murmured agreement from a church pew in my pink starched dress and black patent leather shoes. At night, I slept below a brass-and-wood crucifix with a dried Easter palm tucked behind it. A porcelain figure of a black-robed nun stood on my dresser, a reminder of fifth-grade aspirations to join the Sisters of Notre Dame with their mysterious, waist-length veils. I made my First Communion at St. Paul's Church, took Hope as my confirmation name at St. Stephen's, and carefully studied my illustrated book of the lives of saints and martyrs. The slender, remote pastor who presided over our parish—which was dominated by families like ours with large broods of children—eventually died of AIDS.

The Gothic romance of death was part of growing up. The nuns would tell us tales of deathbed conversions, of martyrs and missionaries and tiny babies saved from limbo with trickles of holy water. I remember pressing Sister Mary Jean Therese about the protective qualities of the stamp-size cotton scapular with a picture of Jesus and his glowing heart that we wore around our necks below forest green plaid uniforms. If we wore them every day, we were assured we would reach heaven.

"If you were really a bad person but still wore it every day, could you get into heaven?" I asked, probing for weak spots in the logic. I had no clue at the time that the scapular was a small, symbolic version of the scapulars worn by monks and nuns as a sign of humility during the Middle Ages.

"You could try, but God is all-knowing. The scapular would burn so terribly that you would tear it from your neck," Sister Mary Jean Therese said. She smiled at me, her long wooden pointer stick at her side. Under the tutelage of the Sisters of Notre Dame, we learned practical lessons for Catholic emergencies such as sprinkling water as a last act of baptism, suitable for Catholics, Protestants, and pagans (who could qualify only for purgatory, but still, it was better than hell).

Nobody in any of our discussions about faith ever mentioned Jews. Eventually, we learned about the selfless acts of the martyrs of the New Testament, immortalized in picture books that I took home to pore over at night with a flashlight in my bed. My most fundamental religious debate was whether I would rather demonstrate my faith by dying naked on the frozen tundra or suffering the flames at the stake. I calculated that it would take longer to freeze on the ice, so I leaned toward burning.

All of my pondering about identity had brought me back to the question that I grappled with since I was a child. What does it mean to be Catholic? I could not resist the emotional pull of the history and rituals of the Catholic Church, although long ago I drifted away from attending Sunday mass and listening to the priests' homilies. Still, I treasured the rich memories of the lacy white Communion veils of my youth, the pink rosary beads I was given, and the dark, hushed confessionals I would enter every week to confess my sins through a screen to an unseen but all-forgiving priest. I would remain a Catholic, but one defined by the non-Catholic world where I felt more comfortable.

So it intrigued me when my newspaper byline inspired people to write letters questioning the origin of my name, Carvajal. While I ignored the most elemental symbol in my life, others constantly pushed me to take notice. A letter writer from Israel sent a handwritten note while vacationing in the United States to ask whether I was related to a long-lost Jewish friend of hers, Dorothy Carvajal. While researching a story in Philadelphia, a rabbi from a local Sephardic synagogue told me my family name had Jewish origins with roots in the Iberian Peninsula. One day I ate lunch with a Long Island philosophy professor for a story I was working on about corruption at his university. During the interview, he posed the same question about my family past. In Madrid many years later, I shared a similar conversation with a top Spanish newspaper editor and former broadcast journalist who discovered the Jewish roots of his name from a medieval studies professor while on a Nieman Fellowship at Harvard.

"Do you know," another reader wrote to me after one of my stories from Spain was published, "that your last name is the same as a family of secret Jews burned at the stake in Mexico in the sixteenth century?"

For most of my life, I paid scant attention to my family tree beyond the fresh, green leaves that surrounded me. My father generally avoided talking about his own father, who had been absent for most of his life. And when he did bring my grandfather up, my father always held him at arm's length, referring to El Gato simply as "your grandfather." By the time Grandfather died in March 2000 at age ninety-two, they had maintained the silence between them for more than fifty years.

I was the only one among the six siblings who met El Gato. I can't fully explain what drove me, but back in the 1980s I decided to spend a summer in Costa Rica. The pretext was to improve my Spanish in a special immersion school and to get to know relatives I barely knew or had never met— including uncles and aunts who were the children of my grandfather's second and third wives. Perhaps it was the beginning of finding my way back to where I belonged.

The first time I met El Gato, I could see the occasional fierceness of my father's green eyes in his direct gaze. He was a shrunken old man by then, but still loved his daily rum and Coke, an occasional cigarette held aloft in his bony fingers, and lunch at the swank refuge of Costa Rica's elite, the private Club Union. The waiters there still called him Dr. Carvajal. He tried to make up for decades of lost time by constantly stuffing the local currency, Costa Rican *colones*, in my hand. In retrospect, that was the time to ask many questions. But I didn't, reluctant to tread on the lost relationship between father and son. We never really talked much about religion, though he made it clear he had no use for churches.

But mostly I remembered the sadness I felt when he talked to me about his dreams of my father, who forever remained a young boy to him.

I started asking questions about El Gato and our family's identity after I had settled in France in 2002. I think my earlier move to Europe—and the feelings of rootlessness it provoked—must have stirred my curiosity about our family and our past. Eventually, I wrote letters to my father's cousin Cecilia, seeking information about our family, and in 2003 got her answer about our Sephardic past. She was a vivacious free spirit whose father was once the Costa Rican ambassador to Mexico and whose wife left him for a prosperous professor. Cecilia moved briefly to San Francisco and became entranced by the Beat generation in the 1950s in North Beach. There she met a man, was married to him for a few days, bore his son, and then did something unheard of at the time: she divorced him and moved back to Costa Rica to raise her son by herself.

There were a few minor challenges. Her son did serve some time in jail for blowing up a statue of John F. Kennedy in the Costa Rican capital of San José, but everyone blamed that adventure on youthful excess.

I moved in with Cecilia for a summer in 1989 to immerse myself in Spanish and got a crash course in our quirky family history. I suppose I was seeking something even then, but I wasn't asking the right questions. Cecilia never had much money, but she welcomed me into her little apartment in San José, where I also dabbled with the idea that this country might feel like home. That didn't happen, but it wasn't long before she became my family oracle.

She somehow managed to be a consummate traveler on a very tight budget well into her seventies. She died of a heart attack a day after she had celebrated her arrival in Mexico with a late-night fiesta.

Not even death stopped her travels. The urn containing her ashes mysteriously disappeared from a baggage rack while her middle-aged son was riding on a Costa Rican bus headed to the suburbs from San José. The tiny nation's most widely read tabloid, *Diario Extra*, featured a photograph of her miserable son appealing for the return of her ashes and the blunt headline "They Stole Mama on the Bus." Two days later, the shamed thief dropped off the urn with a cleaning lady for the bus company, in time for the family's memorial service to scatter the ashes by the bright blue Pacific.

As the family prepared for Cecilia's memorial, I remembered one of the last conversations I had with her, a couple of years before she died, when she came to see me in France. We were sitting on a rumbling train, passing along the placid green river Oise. I had already dispensed with all the gossip about different branches of the family and Cecilia was leaning back against the train seat with her eyes half closed.

"Why did we forget that we were Jews?" I asked.

"The older generations didn't forget," Cecilia laughed. "It was just a subject they avoided."

"But we lost something."

"Listen to me," she said, gazing toward the river. "Maybe they saved themselves."

NINE

Sharp Notes

Arcos de la Frontera, 2008

Two families occupy the old Inquisition jail on the steep slope of Calle de Leal in Arcos de la Frontera. Since the nineteenth century, the jail has served as an unassuming home with only a large iron lantern to mark its battered oak door. In this house Manolo "Zapata" Gallardo Téllez was born in 1912.

The name meant nothing to me when I first arrived in Arcos and glimpsed a bronze bust of Zapata wearing a gaucho cowboy hat and presiding over a little plaza, gazing at the circling cars with a crooked smile. But in flamenco and singing circles, Zapata was a towering name, a voice of ancient grief for his ability to sing Semana Santa *saeta* music in the ancient style of Franciscan monks and Jewish cantors. He was carrying on a tradition of his working-class family, who carried the nickname Zapata because they worked as hands on a ranch of that name, taming Andalusian horses.

When Zapata sang his first *saeta* as a young boy at dawn on a Good Friday, he stunned his father, a *saeta* singer himself, who had no idea his son could perform. Somewhere he soaked up the sighing and rising notes of the Kol Nidre—a haunting Jewish prayer sung during Yom Kippur—and the Gregorian tones of *salmodia remota*—infinite emotion.

Perhaps his secret inspiration came from spirits. He often told his family that something—or someone—was buried under his home in the former Inquisition jail. If white walls and stones could cry, maybe they gave Zapata the force that García Lorca called *duende*, "a mysterious power that all may feel and no philosophy can explain."

It cannot be a coincidence that Zapata raised his voice during the darkest days of Spain under Franco, who led a pariah nation haunted by food rationing, strict censorship, and Civil War executions that left a legacy of hundreds of secret mass graves. Only recently have researchers and historians dared to unearth mass graves across Spain. At least six are in Arcos de la Frontera, which was taken by rebel forces in July 1936 and became an important zone to attack Franco's Nationalists in the mountain region. The systematic executions of Republican rebel forces around Arcos continued until 1942, when the last of the fighters were conquered.

By seeking out elderly people to plumb their memories

of that time, researchers established that there were at least five mass graves—one they described as enormous—dug in trenches and then cemented over in the town's municipal cemetery of San Miguel. A sixth lies in a pit off the road between Arcos and the pueblo of El Bosque, near a little stream. Archaeologists and historians, working in the wider region of the province of Cádiz, suspect that there are many more mass graves in Arcos de la Frontera.

Given the brutality and killings that it endured on the frontier for centuries, Arcos evolved as a hub for the *saeta*, a mystical expression of Andalusian culture marked by raw emotion. The residents of Arcos live, after all, in daily contact with the spirits of the dead.

Saetas are performed with slight differences in each region and the oldest and most primitive are believed to be in Arcos. Manolo Zapata mastered the rarest, most ancient form, the Saetas Viejas de Arcos de Frontera, which few contemporary *saeta* singers are able to perform.

I first heard some recordings of the haunting voice of Manolo Zapata in neighboring Jerez de la Frontera at a special flamenco museum, Centro Andaluz de Flamenco. It is housed in an eighteenth-century mansion with a tiled baroque-rococo courtyard where concerts are sometimes performed. The museum's aim is to save the voices of singers like Zapata in a library where visitors can huddle at wooden desks and listen to old recordings or watch videos of flamenco dances from a vast archive. The museum also houses the memorabilia of dresses, mantillas, and shoes.

Zapata's voice did not disappoint me. I watched him in a video, singing with his lopsided smile, his leathery face deeply lined. Weaving his voice around mournful notes, he started softly, in an echoing melody that became louder and more forceful, ordering listeners to pay attention.

I couldn't understand how he developed such a distinctive style or how he made a direct link with vanished voices, a technique I could use myself to reach the ghosts of my own family. So I decided to search for his secret inspiration, tracking down his son Manuel Gallardo Barroso, who has moved not far from the Inquisition jail. He was also part of the pueblo's bustling cultural industry, a poet, painter, and singer, and a self-taught restorer of medieval sculptures of images paraded by most of the pueblo's Holy Week *cofradías*, including his own, the Brotherhood of Silence.

It wasn't hard to find Manuel Gallardo Barroso. Friends of friends directed me to a *palacio* in Arcos de la Frontera that in its glory days belonged to a long-vanished family of rich aristocrats headed by the Marqués de Torresoto. All I knew was that the *palacio* was footsteps from the church of San Pedro and the Plaza del Caño, where Inquisition trials were once staged. They didn't know the address, but they described a little plaza and a cracked blue-and-yellow tile embedded in the white wall of the palace that was a mark of the *familiares*, the enforcers of the Inquisition.

I left a note in the vestibule beyond the wide double doors and also called Manuel, who readily agreed to meet me. I didn't know quite what to expect when I rang his bell, but he immediately welcomed me into the courtyard of the *palacio,* lush with potted palms and ferns.

He was pleased to talk about his father, proud to show yellowing brochures when Zapata performed his *saetas* in churches in France, where he had staged church concerts five times. Manuel's voice grew husky when he talked about him, even though he had died years earlier, in 1990.

Eventually, our conversation veered to the Inquisition jail and the life of his father in the boxy white house. "Surely it had some effect on his music," I said, "because he sang in such an ancient style."

That was understatement. No one has been able to imitate Zapata's *saetas* since he died, although others have tried to reclaim his style of singing "old *saetas,*" which were based on synagogue chants.

Manuel pondered my question about family history in the Inquisition jail. But every time he started to answer, it seemed to me that some hidden force seemed to interrupt him. "My father always had a tremendous obsession . . ."

The bells of San Pedro started thundering so loudly that it was as if the notes had joined our conversation in Manuel's courtyard. He paused to let the bells speak, drawing rainwater in a bucket from an ancient *pozo* to water his jungle of potted plants. Then he resumed the thread of his thought, smiling as he recalled one of his father's enduring fixations.

"He had a tremendous obsession that below one part of the house there was something in a hole," Manuel told me.

"And was there something?"

"The truth is that we had work done to put in a new floor and we didn't find anything."

"Did he think he could feel the spirits of people who had lived there?"

"No, I don't know exactly. It was just his sensation that under this house there had to be something."

"Treasure? Riches? History?"

"I don't know. Perhaps there were skeletons or . . . I don't know."

I noticed that Manuel started to add something else, then stopped. But I had just met him. It was impossible for me, a foreigner, to push too hard in a second language. I lacked the delicate fluency to probe in a diplomatic way. So I tried another subject.

"What was the influence of Jews on *saeta* music?" I asked him. "I've read that *saeta* music dates back to conversos in the sixteenth century who would sing to demonstrate their faith to the Catholic Church."

"Yes, perhaps there are elements. Maybe the Arabs, too," he answered me vaguely, referring to the influence of the Moors.

Manuel spoke from experience. He sang *saetas* himself in the streets of Arcos during Semana Santa. But he made his living as a sculptor, tending the ancient religious images carried in religious processions. When I visited him, his gauzy watercolor of the church belfry of San Pedro was propped half-finished against a frame with a paintbrush lying against a pallet. Medieval images of Mary and Jesus beckoned in darkened rooms off the courtyard, awaiting repairs.

When Manuel talked about his father, his voice betrayed a fleeting tremor before he cleared his throat. Other *saeteros* have the same habit when they talk about loved ones who have died. Perhaps it's a habit of unleashing emotions in music. From listening to Manuel speak, it was difficult to know.

The *saetas* are performed differently in every town in Spain, but Arcos lays claim to performing the oldest and most primitive forms. Over time, the *saeta* music takes its toll on singers who perform unaccompanied. Some performers strain their vocal cords. Others live on the edge, such as Antonio, a second-generation *saetero* whom I have seen perform and who is known for his *quejios*—deep laments or flamenco cries of *ah ah aheeee* that are a mark of "new *saetas*." I never met him in person, but he lives not far from Manuel. On weekdays, Antonio serves a drug sentence at the local prison. On weekends, he sings at local clubs.

For Manuel, the burden of *saetas* was psychological. A moment came in his singing career when the emotional toll was too much for him to chant.

"The truth is that after my father died, singing *saetas* produced memories of such sorrow and emotion that I couldn't sing them anymore," Manuel explained to me. "It's really difficult to sing because of the Gregorian influence. You have to struggle with the words deep in your throat."

Eventually, he transformed that struggle into writing

lyrics for *saetas*, composing dozens inspired by the images. In his workshop, he has restored various Madonna statues, from the Virgin of Anguish to Nuestra Señora de los Dolores, a sumptuous eighteenth-century image that carries a golden heart in her hand. The heart is pierced by seven gilded daggers, a symbol of her seven sorrows, from the flight to Egypt to receiving the body of Christ.

It is Manuel's job to tend the statue for the brotherhood's four hundred members. Before each procession, in a complicated ritual with another aide, he dresses the statue in embroidered robes and handmade lace. And he walks alongside the *paso* to check her progress during the procession.

"I didn't learn this from anybody. I learned this on my own with a lot of anguish and effort," Manuel said. "I like taking care of images because they are works of art."

Yet he still composes *saeta* lyrics, some gathered in a slim, self-published book dedicated to his father. He always has it on hand, ready to read aloud when the mood strikes him. After I had talked to him for about an hour, he startled me to make a point by reading a passage in his deep silky voice.

"The pain of a saetero / Is to fail to sing. / Because he knows his luck / Is a song of prayer / That is praying twice."

How did the *saeta* evolve? Most experts agree that the early primitive form of *saeta* was composed of Gregorian psalms sung by friars and monks during missions. Later the musical structure broke free and was adapted for singing in the street, reshaped by converso Jews in the sixteenth century. Typically it is sung now with five fragments of lyrics, a *quinta*, with great similarities to the fourteenth- and fifteenth-century versions of the Kol Nidre. The prayer is a message beseeching God to annul religious promises made in the last year.

One theory holds that *saetas* emerged as a subversive form of singing that allowed converso Jews to demonstrate passion for their new religion while communicating despair to insiders who could decode their desperate choice: baptism, exile, or death.

The lyrics dwell almost as much on the suffering of the singer as it does on the pain of Christ and the sorrow of the Virgin Mary.

"¿Quién me presta una escalera?" is from a classic *saeta* song, asking, "Who will give me a ladder to free Christ from the cross?" That poses a double meaning about flight from a world of sorrow and union with God.

In the villages of Andalusia, the *saeta* allowed generations of men and women to raise their voices from little wrought-iron balconies or in the street. Anyone could sing the popular street form—even hardened prison convicts. When religious images were paraded past jails, Spanish prisoners adopted *saetas* again to sing *carceleras*, or jailhouse songs. "Pressed against the bars of the jail, when the one from Nazareth passed by, I shouted at him: Jesus of my soul, and immediately I was free of guilt."

The political power of the *saeta* was so potent that it was effectively stifled during the early 1930s when the government of the Second Republic sought to control the power of the Catholic Church by banning religious processions. Rebels fought back with the sharp notes and little arrows of *saetas*.

Among them was Miguel Cambaya, who, according to local legend, defied the ban along with a local brotherhood, Nuestro Padre Jesús Nazareno, which had been marching in Arcos de la Frontera since 1589. The brothers, dressed in coarse brown tunics, paraded through the streets in silence, despite threatened reprisals. While headed down Calle de la Corredera, the main street that runs like a vein through Arcos, no one noticed Cambaya standing at a balcony, overlooking the procession. There Cambaya shattered the tense quiet with wails of *ahieee ahieee* and a five-line *saeta* of reproach.

"They say Spain is not Christian in the local bank and although it is Republican, it is you, God, who sent us by the light of dawn."

The burst of applause was so loud that in that moment the *saeta* returned to Arcos de la Frontera, never to vanish again.

Defiance is the essence of Andalusians, who call on miracles in everyday life to deliver them. For centuries, the *saeta* has been used to beseech God in a hostile environment. As we talked about the power of *saetas*, Manuel mentioned to me a *saeta* singer who was praying for a miracle. She had damaged her vocal cords while singing the taxing *saeta* music and she had not sung for four years.

I was intrigued. The *saeta* was the music of the dispossessed, of Jewish conversos who tried to break their silence and leave a legacy of subversive music. Here was a woman who had lost her voice and was trying to find it. Perhaps she was my guide to reach another realm.

"How can I find her?"

"Her name is Mari. You can find her in her bakery. I will call her for you."

TEN

Clues in the Blood

Paris, 2009

Sometimes one story suffices for a family or a generation. But the puzzle of identity so nagged me that I tried to resolve it by collecting masses of information. Some of it was confusing, some of it banal, some useful. My persistent, sometimes even frantic digging stemmed from my desire to know the answer to a basic question: If we don't know the truth about our past, then who are we?

To seek my answers, I shifted into investigative reporter mode. In my job I traffic in words. That's the currency, my coin of the realm. I hunt for facts, chase down people to listen to what they have to say, absorb what their thoughts are, and distill it. Over the three decades that I've been a journalist, I have grown confident that anything can be tracked, across distance and time, through people and places.

When my brother-in-law, Dennis, and sister, Pat, in California faced the heartbreaking realization that he suffered from esophageal cancer, I set up my laptop computer on my kitchen table and began to pore through medical studies, searching for information that offered hope. I learned about blackberry powder that helped reduce the cancer in laboratory rats. For good measure, I also tracked down an *herboristerie*—a vintage herbal store established in the nineteenth century—that sold natural remedies to attack cancer: the extract from the neem tree in India to fight free radicals and a liquid from Peru to boost his immunity.

We all prayed, including me, despite my own doubts and religious ambivalence. I lit a candle at a hillside chapel in a white village in Spain dedicated to Our Lady of Remedies, who is the patron saint of the pueblo. Why not? They said that she wiped out a drought and vanquished the plague. I didn't care which religion offered a miracle, and in the face of life and death, identity didn't seem to matter as much. Then one morning I received an e-mail from my sister with the latest test results: after several rounds of chemotherapy, the cancer was receding from his bones.

"I don't know what you are doing," the cancer specialist told my older sister, who is a nurse, "but keep doing it."

I followed the same philosophy with my own family sleuthing. I just kept on looking. My labors are not very different from the métier of Arcos's *cronista*, Don Manuel. All the joys and misfortunes of the ancient quarter passed through the clacking keys of his old Royal typewriter.

I envied Don Manuel and his work; I was having trouble filling up a slim reporter's notebook about my family's past. I needed more facts, more words, to fill in the gaps of my family's memory about a discarded Sephardic identity. I knew others had succeeded in quests similar to mine. Over the last twenty-five years, this kind of arcane history has been excavated by amateurs and academics who have made a field of mining information about the secret past of crypto-Jews, as they are called in the United States.

In the Southwest, where many Latino families in Arizona and New Mexico trace their origins to Spain, there are yearly academic conferences that offer eclectic exhibitions of crypto-Jewish glassware and Sephardic music concerts. Among the panels are theoretical seminars such as "Juggling Identities: Identities and Authenticity Among Crypto-Jews," "Identity Coercion Shaped by Religious Rigidity," "Doña Jimena: Parallels with Models of Crypto-Jewish Femininity," and "Virgin of Guadalupe—Christian or Jew?"

Within this eclectic group mingles Roger Martinez, a boyish and enthusiastic assistant professor of history at the University of Colorado at Colorado Springs. His easy charm and relentless curiosity serve him well when hunting for yellowed documents in ancient churches of Spain. Somehow, wary Catholic priests lay aside their suspicions of strangers when this strapping, curly-haired Texan presents himself in fluent Spanish with a professor's identity card and engaging manner. Some have even entrusted him with the keys to church archives stacked with records that date back to the fifteenth century. Martinez's specialty involves decoding the cramped, slanted handwriting of medieval scribes, analyzing wills, dowry letters, church records, legal pleas, and royal correspondence.

One of Martinez's early passions was the Carvajal Genetic Genealogy Project. Essentially he tried to organize an international database of DNA to track genetic information about the wandering Carvajal families from Spain, Portugal, the Canary Islands, Mexico, South America, and Texas, California, and New Mexico. His goal was to determine genetic links among the Diaspora of Sephardic Jews and to study how they had scattered across the world. He was looking for clues to determine whether converso Jewish families had purposely clung to each other, intermarrying within closed groups across different countries in a covert strategy to hold on to their secret faith. His own Carvajal lineage is from San Antonio, Texas, through relatives who arrived in the New World between 1700 and 1710 when a soldier named Mateo de Carvajal settled in the newly formed Villa de San Antonio de Béjar, which is now San Antonio.

I met Professor Martinez in Paris while he was there on vacation with his wife. When we gathered for dinner in a nineteenth-century brasserie of stained glass and mahogany near the old Paris stock exchange, he told me about his own ongoing effort to track Carvajal lines. He hit a dead end with

Inquisition records in Madrid because the family appeared well placed enough to avoid prosecution.

"This is a very, very tricky subject," he said. "Basically, I've identified only one or two Carvajal families that were fully investigated by the Inquisition. The case was ultimately dropped, as the inquisitors didn't seem to validate their claims regarding a problematic genealogy for these Carvajals. As you know, the Inquisition operated on a regional basis—and I don't think there were any Carvajals pursued in Madrid.

"Another item that you might take into consideration is the absence of Inquisition files—perhaps due to the Carvajal influence over ecclesiastical and royal institutions."

Over a dinner of duck Parmentier and Bordeaux, he encouraged me to try genetic testing as part of my research. But I wasn't sure what the family reaction would be to that suggestion. It was clear that other Carvajals seemed wary, too, since only a few dozen volunteers had agreed to allow their DNA results to be included in his project.

"You need to ask your father to take a DNA test," he pressed me.

"But what if he won't do it?"

"Well, I've had my own difficulties in my family, but you have to try. Don't lose that chance."

I understood what Roger meant from personal experience. I greatly regretted the questions I had failed to ask, the curiosity that vanished when it came to my own family. How many times I wished I could call my grandmother, Mamita, to ask questions about revealing family rituals.

At that point, Roger told me a personal story of his own ongoing efforts to persuade some of his own Carvajal relatives to take a DNA test for his research.

"Were you ever successful?" I asked him again after he returned to the United States and was working on a history book tracing the path of Carvajals who moved to colonial Bolivia, Peru, and Argentina.

"I could not convince my Carvajal male relatives to participate," he replied in an e-mail. "It's been frustrating. But that's the way it is."

His own personal DNA search turned up the unexpected. It showed that his genetic signature had Native American roots on both sides of his family. That "speaks to the limitations of DNA," he said. "In spite of our oral history, there is little left to bind us to our past."

I really didn't expect much of a eureka moment of self-discovery. So I ordered a DNA test, on sale for $99 from a Texas company, and mailed it to my father in California.

"Would you mind doing this?" I asked my father with a little trepidation. What if he said no to me? I could track the same male line of DNA with help from my two brothers, but I would lose the chance for information about the line of my grandmother, Mamita. It was just one clue in the kaleidoscope of family, a collection of shards: family memories, religious practices, talismans of Jewish faith, and adopted countries.

But I decided to bet on history, which is carried in our genes. DNA—deoxyribonucleic acid—is a double-stranded helical molecule in the cells of all organisms. It carries the genetic instructions to build an organism and controls cell functions. These biological heirlooms are passed down, unchanged, from parent to child with genetic markers on the Y chromosome passed by fathers and mitochondrial DNA passed by mothers.

In the nuclear DNA of males, the Y chromosome is nearly identical among sons, fathers, grandfathers, and male cousins for generations. It offers genetic marker results that are expressed as a set of numbers called a haplotype, which distinguishes one male line from another.

The allure of these haplogroups and DNA testing is that it offers the appearance of simplicity. With the world divided into an alphabet pool of haplogroups, my hope is that it will codify reality to make it manageable. An individual transforms into a formula of sequences numbered in series of DYS markers totaling 12, 25, 37, 43, or 67. Over the centuries they interact, sometimes colliding, sometimes not.

In their published research study, European geneticists Francesc Calafell, of the Pompeu Fabra University in Barcelona, and Mark Jobling, of the University of Leicester in England, set out to explore the genetic legacy in Spain of Jews and Moors, two groups that shared the bitter fate of exile, conversion, and Church-sanctioned executions during the Spanish Inquisition. Their findings were intriguing, for they revealed a high level of conversions: there was evidence that 19.6 percent of living Spanish men are descended from Sephardic Jews, and another 10.6 percent carry the genetic signature of Moors. If the study had included women, the percentages would likely have been pushed even higher. Their study was based on an analysis of Y chromosomes gathered from 174 DNA samples from Sephardic men in communities where Jews migrated in streams from Spain after 1492, such as communities in Portugal, Greece, Turkey, and Bulgaria. They also developed similar signatures for the Y chromosomes of Arabs and Berbers by gathering samples from men in Morocco and the Western Sahara. Then they compared that data against DNA samples from 1,140 men from all of Spain's regions.

Dr. Calafell's own Y chromosome—from the G haplogroup—may be of Sephardic ancestry. This genetic set of markers on the male line has a low frequency in most of the world's populations. His DNA samples from Sephardic men showed that the most prevalent haplotypes, or genetic markers, were J1, J2, and G. His surname is inspired by a town in Catalonia, an intriguing clue to his possible background because there were theories that converso Jews often took surnames from places and animals. But his Y chromosome is not definitive proof. As he noted, "My full ancestry is made of many different individuals, and my Y chromosome tells me just about one of them." He told me, "My haplotype is quite rare. It may have originated in the Near East and have come to Iberia with the Jews or the Phoenicians, but humans do move also as individuals beyond historic migrations." His DNA on his mother's side, by contrast, is from a family that never strayed far from the same villages in Spain. The same DNA "has been found in a skeleton dug from a three-thousand-year-old Neolithic archaeological site just sixty kilometers [thirty-seven miles] away from my hometown. I know that seven out of my eight great-grandparents were born in a ten-kilometer [six-mile] radius," he said.

A friend in Mexico, Federico Garza Martínez, an amateur historian, advised me to keep looking for a narrative to connect the dots. "DNA is a helpful way to find clues, nothing conclusive," he said. "It only tells you your paternal and maternal lines—two points among millions. I promote other fronts because you descend from many people. Sometimes the most promising clues are unexpected—like an out-of-wedlock ancestor."

In effect, I was making a mosaic, moving colored tiles around until a clear picture emerged. In some Spanish communities, such as the island of Mallorca, descendants of Jewish conversos can trace their family trees back five hundred years with the indefatigable help of inquisitors who kept careful records of trials.

An Israeli group, Shavei Israel—which means "Israel returns"—dispatched roving rabbis to countries where converso descendants show interest in learning more about their origins and religion. So far they have fanned out to Spain, Portugal, Brazil, China, Poland, and southern Italy and Sicily in search of what they call "lost Jews."

Michael Freund, a New York native and former deputy

director of communications in the prime minister's office for Benjamin Netanyahu, founded the organization to "cultivate that connection that people have with their identity."

"Some are looking to convert and the organization provides a special school in Israel for that purpose. But others— who have no interest in organized religion and are happy living in Spain or Portugal or wherever—might simply have an emotional curiosity that their ancestors were once Jews," he told me.

When I first contacted Michael, I fell in the second category, avoiding any kind of a religious commitment, never entering the doors of a synagogue once in my life. I felt very reserved about the issue and was poised to cut off discussion if Michael broached religious conversion. But he scrupulously avoided the subject, and I was grateful, because I didn't have the answers.

I knew that Michael's politics were clearly conservative after reading a sampling of his columns for the English-language *Jerusalem Post* that supported the expansion of Israeli settlements in Judea and Samaria. But his approach with his organization is delicate, providing information in a neutral way. When I contacted him, the group was in the midst of preparing a how-to book for people researching buried family secrets of Jewish origin.

"I thought that Jews avoid proselytizing for converts," I said to Michael. "What's the difference with what your group is doing?"

"We do not proselytize," Michael said, "but of course it's

a thin line. The difference is that more and more people are looking to reclaim their Jewish roots. In many instances they are met with hostility or suspicion. They have no place to turn. So we try to fill that void."

I had never faced any hostility because I had too many doubts to step forward forcefully to reclaim a religion. But Michael and his group offered what I thought was a no-commitment spiritual journey by simply offering information. The group was working in Poland, where a number of children and grandchildren of Holocaust survivors faced dramatic discoveries about their secret Jewish identities, which were hidden during World War II.

One was a Polish priest, Romuald Waszkinel, who, in his thirties, in a conversation with his adoptive Catholic mother when she was on her deathbed, learned that his real name was Jakub Weksler. She had raised him for his Jewish mother, Batia, to protect him from the Nazis. His search for his identity and his journey to Israel were the subject of a documentary, *Torn*.

The ultimate example of a seeker is Pawel, an anti-Semitic Polish skinhead who discovered his hidden Jewish roots in Poland and transformed himself into an Orthodox Jew. A friend of mine, Daniel Bilefsky, interviewed him, recounting his story for the *International Herald Tribune* and *The New York Times*. His secret origins were a legacy of World War II, when many Jews hid their faith in order to survive and guarded their secrets to fit in within heavily Catholic communities. Pawel discovered his origins when his wife researched her own family's background in genealogical records along with his relatives'. To their astonishment, she found both sets of their grandparents on a register of Warsaw Jews.

Pawel confronted his parents, who explained the family tragedy: His maternal grandmother, who was Jewish, survived World War II by hiding in a convent, sheltered by nuns. His grandfather, also a Jew, lost most of his seven brothers and sisters in the Holocaust. For weeks, Pawel couldn't look at himself in the mirror, and he told Dan that he sought solace from a rabbi, who explained his anguish: "The sleeping souls of your ancestors are calling out to you."

It was Dan, who is Jewish and from Montreal, who encouraged me to keep looking for my own clues.

"You have a Jewish soul," he joked with me on one of his swings through Paris when we stopped for espressos at a sidewalk café near the river Seine. "That would explain your maternal instinct to offer solutions for every problem, however small, and your irrational love of Middle Eastern food, and your sense of justice, which is a very Talmudic thing."

"Next thing you know, you will tell me that my chicken soup is proof of origins," I replied. "I need something concrete that will erase all my doubts." My hope was that DNA clues could give me a clear picture of my family's past. I had no dusty, magical trunk that I could open to find a hoard of letters that would offer answers. In 2008, I wrote to Stanley Hordes, a historian in New Mexico who has traced the history of crypto-Jews and described a long process of digging:

probing baptismal, marriage, burial, and Inquisition records and looking for patterns.

I asked him about tracing our family branches and, in particular, asked whether there could be any link to the Carvajal family tried by the Inquisition in Nuevo León in Mexico.

"Your story sounds compelling," he wrote back in an encouraging note. But he added that "Carvajal (or Carvalho in Portuguese) was not an uncommon name on the Iberian Peninsula, and it cannot automatically be assumed that there was a familial link."

For family sleuths like me, he offered a checklist of advice to embark on a quest for clues. Were there signs of endogamy—converso Jews marrying among other converso Jews—in the families? Was there a job pattern that allowed men to wander among hospitable countries, and a receptive network of other secret Jews? Did families use biblical names like Esther or Samuel?

The majority of conversos were merchants and peddlers who were international traders, relying on trusted connections with other crypto-Jews in the American colonies and openly European Jews, especially from the Netherlands.

I kept searching for family records from Costa Rica, running into roadblocks. Initially, I could not request copies of church birth, marriage, and death records in Costa Rica— the only documents that go back through the centuries I needed—without hiring a local lawyer. Sitting in Europe, I searched online and picked a bilingual lawyer, Gregory, who advertised his expertise in probing the genealogical past in Costa Rica. I was skeptical about relying on a lawyer who advertised his eclectic services for gathering genealogical records and organizing wedding ceremonies at the same time he boasted about his previous career highlight—as a Beverly Hills paparazzo—with photos of himself with Michael Jackson. Despite my misgivings, I wired him $600 and received a polite acknowledgment.

I didn't get much else from him for five months. By the time I heard from my paparazzo lawyer again, I had already pressed forward on my own research, thanks to a pilot project of American Mormons who recruited legions of dedicated volunteers to travel through tiny Central American nations to photograph church records and then post them online.

What an eerie delight it was to see, with a few clicks of a computer keyboard, names of my ancestors written in an elegant sloping hand. The records also revealed long-forgotten family friends listed as godparents on baptismal certificates, and they showed me that my great-grandmother died within hours of her sister, both in their forties. That would explain what happened to my grandmother Mamita at age seventeen. I remembered hazy details about how my grandmother's "second mother"—Albertina Pérez Carvajal—had scooped young Angela into her family in almost a tribal way, marrying her off six months later to her handsome second son, José Francisco Carvajal. The birth and burial records I found also showed the occupations on both sides of the family. The women typically were housewives, the men merchants or politicians. One was a mayor, or *jefe político*, of San Ramón.

One of the strangest records that found its way to me was produced by the paparazzo lawyer, who dug up a *dispensa*, or marriage petition, sought in 1869 by my great-great-grandfather José Carvajal. There were testimonies of support from local businessmen to the good character of José and his future bride, Petronilla Alvarado.

As it turned out, José needed the *dispensa* because his bride was his fourth cousin, according to my Costa Rican lawyer. They were carrying on in a grand family tradition, the records showed. Petronilla's parents—my great-great-great-grandparents Hermengildo Alvarado and Juana Solís— were also fourth cousins.

As I read over the records, I realized that here were some dots that I could connect to a broader pattern that historians had found among the descendants of converso Jews. The men in the Carvajal family had pursued commercial professions as merchants, which allowed them to travel and wander.

The clannish behavior of intermarriage among distant cousins was perhaps a sign of endogamy, which was contrary to Catholic norms. But it was an effective strategy to protect family secrets by marrying among other Sephardic families. In different parts of Spanish colonies, according to researchers, regional churches granted hundreds of ecclesiastical dispensations to allow relatives to marry each other.

They were not the eureka clues that I wanted, and not enough to satisfy me. But I thought back to the words of a father who was pressed for answers about the family's Sephardic heritage, and pondered his simple advice.

Don't ask. Think.

ELEVEN

Forbidden Tastes

Arcos de la Frontera, 2008

On the yellow cliffs of Arcos there are dreamers who toil by day as bakers and cooks and late at night cross the *frontera* to their dreams. The border crossing is a local tavern called José de la Viuda, a solid brick storefront more than sixty years old.

Three generations of the Saborido family have run this retreat, which stands across from Plaza Rafael Pérez del Álamo. Local luminaries throng here, from poets and writers to fabled singers with grand titles of flamenco royalty: Camarón de la Isla, Fernando Terremoto, Luis de la Pica, Lole, El Pipa, El Barrio, Jesús Quintero, Juan Luis de Tarifa.

Francisco Saborido is one of the tavern's occasional philosophers, but his day job is to preside over his own hot kitchen and the production of crisp, golden tapas of meat and cheese that he insists are inspired by *trozos*, little fragments of history. Chef Saborido, portly and balding with fashion accessories that vary from a Star of David swinging from his neck to an artfully draped white-and-black Palestinian kaffiyeh, grew up in the swirl of his grandmother's tavern, La Viuda.

I first heard about Francisco from an artist and painter, Jorge, who sips his morning *café solo* in a mansion turned hotel on Calle Corredera that is a gathering place for a younger generation of jazz musicians and writers.

"You're looking for information about *sefarditas*?" Jorge asked one day when we were sharing coffees side by side. "I know exactly the person for you. I warn you, though, he won't stop talking."

Finally, I thought, someone who could help me peer beyond the pueblo's whitewashed walls.

My search for Francisco did not take long. I found him in a dark cave; he was wearing an enormous gold Star of David necklace. The terrace of his restaurant, La Taberna de Boabdil, overlooks the western side of Peña Nueva along La Escalerita, a steep path of stairs that plunges down from Paseo de Boliches and clings to a precipice facing the Guadalete River. When nearby San Miguel church was built on the remains of a synagogue in 1500, the Jewish survivors retreated here to the depths of a seventh-century cave to carry on their rituals in secret, according to Francisco. It provided a quick escape route down the ragged ravine, like other tunnels that lead from houses near my neighborhood of Matrera Abajo on the eastern side of Peña Vieja.

His family has a history of dramatic transformations; Francisco's uncle turned aunt, Manolita Chen—born Manuel Saborido—was the first highly public transsexual in Spain and toured the country as a lithe brunette dancer during the 1960s with her cabaret act, Teatro Chino. She lived near my neighborhood and preferred to be called Elena. Once I left a note of introduction at her door, curious about how she lived openly as a transsexual during the conservative repression of the Franco years. But after a drug arrest in 2004 that led to a conviction and jail sentence in Puerto Santa María, she was as reclusive as Garbo. So I did not expect a response. But when I knocked again for an introduction and she opened the door, she greeted me warmly, kissing both cheeks. She had read my note, but she was not interested in conversation. "I am not doing interviews right now," Manolita/Elena said with the grandeur of her performing days.

"Well, I am going to be here for a while, and I live just up the hill. I will visit again to see if you are ready to talk."

"Of course," she said politely. But every time I knocked after that, no one answered the door.

As a child, Francisco remembered studying the tavern's habitués, like his aunt who came to listen to strains of fla-menco music, somber *soleás* or joyful *bulerías*. It was a time when the people of Spain were squeezed between two powerful forces, the Catholic Church and the Franco regime, according to Francisco. The conservative Catholic government discouraged interest in any Jewish legacy. The Edict of Expulsion of Jews, after all, was not revoked until 1968.

It was a matter of survival and political protection to cover up the past, which is why in Arcos, locals were wary of strangers. They could not talk openly about Jews or Muslims who left their indelible mark on their neighborhoods, where Inquisition tribunals used to reign in the plaza. On their daily walks they ignored the Casa de Angustias, or House of Anguish, on Calle del Camino de Bornos the name of the house referred to the tragedies that befell its owner, Pedro Acosta, a prosperous converso who was accused by his neighbors of "Judaizing" during the Inquisition in 1692.

The mystical seventh-century cave, which Francisco transformed into a restaurant, is the dream that lured him back from his travels as a wandering chef. His goal is to reclaim ancient Sephardic Jewish and Arabic dishes to serve up to contemporary diners. He likes to style himself an archaeologist of cuisine. And I wondered if he could give me a taste of the past that I was seeking.

In his gravelly voice, he has a hypnotic way of describing his journey to this cave, drifting to Marbella, Alicante, Catalonia, and Belgium for almost fifteen years before returning to Arcos. He said his ideas and notions about cuisine didn't make sense to others in his hometown when he left and came back. They couldn't understand why he wanted to reach back to the past to conjure up unfamiliar recipes from forgotten times.

He always was too curious, hovering on the edges of conversations, although when he was a child adults tended to shield him from sensitive information by ordering him to bed.

"When we grew up no one talked about the *sefarditas*, because everyone had fear of the Catholic Church and we lived under Franco," he tells me. "We didn't know there had been Muslims and Jews. Now, of course, we speak more of the culture of Andalusia. Back then older people would talk about secrets in my father's bar. When someone came in whom they wanted to exclude from conversation, they would say, simply, 'Give me some *kpanklá*.'"

I repeat the syllables awkwardly. "*Ka-pahnka-la?*"

"*Kpanklá.*"

It has a satisfying feeling, the powerful knowledge of a secret command for "cover-up." I know the password. It is Andalusian slang for whitewash—*cal para encalar*—an act with profound meaning in Arcos, where seasons are marked by smothering houses with white lime. "We would do it after Christmas, after Semana Santa," Francisco said of his family ritual of applying *cal*. "We did it to clean the houses physically and spiritually. It was a form of purification."

As a teen, it was his hobby to rummage through the junk that people abandoned for garbage collectors along the streets of his neighborhood. He was a fifteen-year-old student when he made a discovery that was of profound importance to him: a huge hand-carved wooden remnant from a synagogue. It was a long horizontal bar of oak, carved in an interlocking pattern of lines and flowers of four petals.

Maybe, he said, it was guarded for centuries by the onetime occupants of a house neighboring his own on Calle del Camino de Bornos, which previously was named Calle de la Cruz Verde, a reference to the signature green cross of the Inquisition.

"I knew right away it was a part of history," Francisco said, sweeping his hand toward his cherished wall. I gazed at the polished carving and together we pondered the notion of home in his cave restaurant, which is named for Boabdil, sultan of the Emirate of Granada, who surrendered the last Muslim city to the Catholic king and queen, Ferdinand and Isabella, in 1492.

The cave's cool interior is a bazaar of battling colors, ragged stone walls painted in mustard, saffron, cinnamon, and deep blue. Overstuffed divans are crowded with fat pillows and along the walls hang copper pots, teakettles, and hand-painted ceramic plates. In the center, Francisco hung the carved wooden remnant from the synagogue in its rightful place, footsteps from the deepest part of the cave where clandestine religious rituals took place. The dusky interior is unused now, silent and hazy with dust and a dirt floor piled with broken furniture.

Over time Francisco simmered his notions of history, culture, and food into his own eclectic philosophy of cuisine that he mixed with childhood memories of his grandmother's cooking. Most people wouldn't care about the distinguishing characteristics of medieval cooking, but with his breathless enthusiasm he is trying to serve a menu at his restaurant that imparts the aromas, tastes, and a little bit of the fear of the forbidden foods of the Inquisition.

"I learned because I asked questions. It's the soul that asks, the heart that demands," Francisco said. "I have always been looking for home. Fifteen years ago I quit the kitchen and lived in many countries because people thought I was crazy like a painter with my ideas."

His eclectic cuisine is also a mélange of the tastes and colors and tribes—as he calls them—of Andalusia. "Tribes like the *sefarditas* and Muslims left a culinary tradition," he said. "All of the Christians here have something Jewish inside of us genetically. It's in our brain or personality and has a way of affecting our thinking, the manner of cooking, the aroma."

I was inclined to dismiss this argument as whimsical storytelling, yet I knew at least a quarter of Andalusians in the western regions carry genes that reflect Sephardic heritage, according to the Spanish geneticist I had interviewed.

"My genetics are Muslim, Jewish, Andalusian," Francisco told me.

"But how do you know this?"

"If you hear rock and roll and feel nothing. If you try something and feel no passion. The mix of Muslims and Jews does something for me. The Saborido in my family was a colonel who was Christian. My maternal grandmother, María Muñoz Huerta, grew up here in the Jewish quarter of San Francisco."

I was not particularly convinced by this, and he noticed my skepticism.

"Look at you, for example, with your American blue eyes and blond hair."

"My grandfather had blue eyes and he lived in Costa Rica," I interrupted him. "The color didn't come from America."

"For that you have a Spanish soul. Your heart is here. I would like to take you on a tour of my old neighborhood. Do you like motorcycles?"

I considered the invitation with trepidation, gazing down to his foot. His ankle was wrapped tight with a bandage—a fresh sprain from tumbling down the steps of the steep Escalerita the night before. I hesitated, picturing a wild, bumpy ride plunging down slippery cobblestone streets. I knew we would cross this *frontera* without helmets and with a nonstop stream of cultural commentary from Francisco. The vision was my equivalent of running with the bulls in Arcos.

Despite my misgivings, I said yes, and we arranged to meet again by his restaurant cave. When I arrived, I spotted his motorcycle—white as lime *cal*—with a leather saddle seat fraying at the edges. He was dressed for the road: aviator sunglasses, black-and-white-checked pants, and clogs.

I worried he would lose them as we rumbled over cobblestones. I gripped his ample waist and we took off with a burst of speed, twisting along steep turns. The narrow passages were so quiet that children played cards in the middle of them, spreading a hand of hearts on the macadam. The purity of Arcos—its whiteness and darkness, its hardness and lightness, the perfect symmetry carved by vanished tribes—resided here.

Over the roar of his motorcycle, he talked in a rush about what lies beyond the whitewash in his childhood neighborhood of Competa, an ancient outpost of steep, winding lanes where Arabs and Jews long ago lived in four streets in the quarter. Among these were Calle de los Mozárabes and Calle de los Sefardíes.

We passed the church of San Francisco, where the Franciscan order of priests presided over the Inquisition. Then we roared toward Calle de Gomeles to a hidden dead-end street where he parked his motorcycle in a lush courtyard filled with potted palms and hanging ivy. The walls were whitewashed and a canary was singing from a plastic birdcage temporarily hanging in a shady corner.

I looked around, trying to absorb the feel of the place, and took out my camera. I was busy taking photographs when suddenly I heard a loud crash and a thud.

I turned to see the motorcycle flopped on the ground and Francisco, with his sprained and bandaged ankle, struggling to raise it upright. Somehow we managed together to retrieve it, though now my misgivings were mounting about pressing on with this tour.

"No te preocupes," he assured me. Don't worry. "Let's keep going. I want to take you to Calle de Matrera Abajo to show you something. There's a nice old doorway inlaid with bones."

It was that kind of breathless and quirky performance that appealed to me about Francisco, who seemed to be more open about Arcos and its history. Perhaps he was too open for his own good.

At one point, when we stopped for a coffee, Francisco confided some doubts about whether people here would accept his notions about reclaiming ancient recipes from painful history. Left unsaid was that for centuries certain recipes were grounds for an Inquisition trial.

"When I proposed offering some Sephardic Jewish cuisine, I thought I might face prejudice," he told me. "I am not an egoist, but I am trying to make something more than a simple restaurant—a global concept with a fusion of ideas."

I sipped my *café solo*, thinking about his cave, which was never crowded. I calculated the diners, usually urban tourists from Madrid and adventurers from Germany or Holland. The little death of any chef is an empty table set with silver forks and pressed napkins. Where were the local diners? Were they avoiding Francisco's restaurant because of the economic crisis gripping Arcos and all of Spain, or was it the exotic flavorings and Francisco's eccentric style? Could it be they felt the weight of history in the cave when certain foods made by Sephardic Jews during the Inquisition constituted evidence of religious crime?

Francisco, ever the provocateur, winked at that with the slogan for his *taberna*—"*El dulce pecado de comer*"—The sweet sin of eating. Spanish Inquisition archives are filled with cases when dietary choices led to jail, exile, or worse. In the fifteenth century, a converso Christian, Beatriz Núñez, was reported to inquisitors by her maid, Catalina Sánchez, who noticed telltale signs of a kosher home. The prime evidence was *adafina*, a fragrant stew whose name means "buried treasure." It's a mix of lamb, chickpeas, and hardboiled eggs stirred with saffron, coriander, ginger, and dates. It could be made on Friday, buried in coals, and eaten on Saturday evening, thus avoiding work on the Sabbath.

For this recipe of *adafina* and other acts of heresy, Beatriz Nuñez was burned alive.

Inquisitors under the directions of the Grand Inquisitor Tomás de Torquemada, who himself had converso origins, collected testimony about Jewish rituals performed in secret. Much of the damning evidence centered on cooking.

On the list of suspicious culinary activities was "not eating pork, hare, rabbit, strangled birds, conger eel, cuttlefish." Preferences for boiled eggs and olive oil roused suspicion. The inquisitors took particular note of whether meat was fried in olive oil instead of lard. Jews typically avoided using lard because it was made from pork.

The hunt for food crimes spread to the Spanish colonies, where inquisitors operated in the urban centers of Peru and Colombia, as well as Mexico City. Trial documents in the archives at the University of California at Berkeley show that some of the evidence against the doomed Carvajal family in Mexico City involved their fasting habits and dietary restrictions. They slaughtered their chickens in the traditional kosher manner, draining the fowl of all blood and then roasting the meat. The records also indicated that they kept a supply of lard in case guests became suspicious.

Within medieval Spain, eating pork demonstrated identity and respect for the Catholic faith. A gift of pork sausage or succulent ham, for example, demonstrated a purity of faith on the part of the giver, as no Muslim or Jew would ever eat such meat. Converted Muslims would offer ham or a slice of salt pork, called a *medalla*—medallion. Some historians argue that Jewish conversos tried so hard to demonstrate their conversion by eating pork that they were given the nickname of Marrano, which means "pig."

Those ancient customs remain deeply ingrained in the national cuisine, and today Spain is one of the world's top consumers per capita of pork, behind only Denmark. The meat dishes dominate menus of humble restaurants and taverns where sides of dried ham dangle as an interior decoration. Madrid offers tourists its museum of ham, where history tells us that clergymen maintained the tradition of raising swine during the Moorish occupation of Spain. When the New World was conquered, priests accompanied the conquistadors and taught Indians about religion and raising pigs. Civilization, after all, is a history of how meats and seeds traveled from place to place. Food teaches about who we are, the fierce politics of the table.

There are more than sixty European saints associated with hogs. The most well known in Spain are San Anton, the abbot, and San Martín, whose feast day, November 11, typically marked the beginning of *matanza*, the ritual slaughter of pigs.

The Spanish national taste for pork is so discriminating

that the most expensive *jamón ibérico* is produced from black Iberian pigs raised in the microclimates of southern Spain in the mountainous regions of the Sierra Morena and Sierra Nevada. They are the most expensive in the world, with the ham that comes from them priced at more than $52 a pound, and $96 a pound for the premium *bellota*. The finest ham comes from free-range hogs that roam in oak groves and graze on a diet of acorns, rosemary, and thyme. The hub of production is in the town of Jabugo, where the town square is named Plaza del Jamón (ham) and the chief producer—which came as a surprise to me—is 5J Sánchez Romero Carvajal.

There is no patriotism deeper or more emotional than gastronomy and there are many ways of saying "pig" in Spanish—*cerdo, cochino, puerco, gorrino, guarro, lechón,* and *marrano*. The vital importance of pork in daily life is best summed up by an old Spanish expression: *"El tocino la olla, el hombre la plaza, y la mujer la casa."* "Everything has its place: salt pork in the pot, the man in the plaza, and the woman in the house."

The deadly politics of cuisine gave rise to insulting nicknames for Jews and conversos in Spanish culture—slurs that endure, mostly variations on "pig" and "pork." *Marrano* is the most common term for descendants of Jewish converts. On the Spanish island of Mallorca, converso descendants are called *chuetas*, which has a variety of interpretations, among them "salted-pork eaters" and "bacon eaters."

Over time, traditional Jewish recipes have been adopted into the national obsession with pork. A coil-shaped challah, which elsewhere is usually reserved for Jewish High Holy Days, is made year-round in Spain as small Mallorcan pastries called *ensaimadas*. In Catalan, *saim* means "lard," and these "larded" pastries are fragments of more history—recipes used by former Jews to demonstrate their conversion.

Today Francisco has incorporated tastes of the forbidden in his tapas. "I don't know where my recipes come from, but I know it comes from my soul, my spirit. It comes from my hands and heart, the memories of my family, the spices that I knew," Francisco said. "I tried to remember how they cooked in my house and the white houses of Arcos."

Sephardic cuisine is a taste of many countries, adopted from cooking in Spain and Portugal under Catholic and Islamic regimes. Cumin, cilantro, saffron, and turmeric are common ingredients. So are caraway and capers, which were brought to Spain by the Muslims. Cinnamon is sometimes used as a meat seasoning, especially in dishes made with ground meat.

For Francisco, those spices are the hunger of memory, vital tools that allowed early explorers to sail out from Cádiz on long voyages of discovery. "The tribes taught us how to preserve foods in salts and spices. Thanks to them, the Americas could be discovered," he said. Despite this legacy, the reception is not always warm for chefs like Francisco who are trying to reclaim Sephardic cuisine. That is partly because of the weight of history and partly because of contemporary politics with left-of-center governments taking a more pro-Palestinian stance.

Janet Amateau, an American chef of Sephardic origins who specializes in Sephardic cuisine, opened her dream restaurant, Tradescantia, on the coast near Barcelona in 2005. To survive, she quickly discovered that she had to disguise the roots of her specialty and learn how to make popular national dishes of pork and shellfish.

"Half the people you meet in Spain look as Jewish as your great-aunt Esther," she said. "Living in modern Spain as a Jew is like living gay among repressed homosexuals. You know it's part of their makeup, and more than a few of them know, too, but they'll be damned if they're ever going to open up to the idea and will turn defensive, nervous, even hostile if you dare broach the subject."

Spain drew her on a holiday vacation that turned into a life-changing shift as a chef. In her spare time, she became a food detective to research Sephardic recipes in their original villages and pueblos around Spain.

"I walk into a store, and little by little I see something that is so clearly Jewish," she said. "There is a psychological connection. Food is so deeply ingrained. I have literally walked down a street in a pueblo, spied something on a table, and thought, 'Oh, that's ours.'"

On the day I spoke to Janet, it was Yom Kippur. I asked her whether she planned to participate.

"I am going to go to work. I don't tell many people anymore that I am Jewish. I can feel the anti-Semitism in the air. In fact, I have a waitress who I get along with really well. One day a customer started revealing her personal life. My waitress said, 'My God, she doesn't even know us. She shouldn't be talking like that. It's like telling a stranger that you're Jewish.' I said, 'What?'"

"So what did her comment mean?"

"Share your secrets only with those people you trust."

"Sounds like my family's strategy."

Since her move to the north of Spain in 2002, Janet has found that the national zest for pork represents a profound link to the past.

"This obsession with pork is a primitive fear so deeply embedded," she said. "Tourists ask me constantly about why the Spanish are so obsessed with pork. It's a mania. To show your Christianity, you had to make a prominent display of eating pork. There are families that to this day have a big old ham hock sitting on the kitchen counter. People had to make Jewish foods un-Jewish by adding pork or lard."

Those attitudes are deeply ingrained in Spain, a legacy of centuries of repression and persecution. Until 2001, the Spanish Royal Academy dictionary included a definition for "synagogue" as a meeting for illicit purposes.

In 2008, the Pew Global Attitudes project conducted a survey in many countries to study how Jews and Muslims are regarded. In Spain, forty-six percent of all Spaniards held negative views of Jews—the highest percentage recorded in any non-Muslim country. Other studies detected similar opinions, although there has been ongoing improvement. The Anti-Defamation League found more than half of those polled in Spain hold anti-Semitic stereotypes about Jewish power, loyalty, and money. A poll commissioned by the Spanish Ministry of Education found that more than fifty percent of students between twelve and eighteen said they would not sit next to a Jew in school. The Israeli embassy in Madrid lodged a formal complaint with Spain after it received dozens of handwritten postcards from school students aged five and six with messages such as "Jews kill for money," "Evacuate the country for Palestinians," and "Go to someplace where someone will be willing to accept you."

These views resonate despite the fact that Jews total only about forty thousand people in a population of forty million. The majority of Jews came from Morocco and Latin America, especially Argentina. Janet has adapted, as others have before her, but she wonders what the cost of amnesia is to the country and culture.

"This nation has not come to grips with its very despicable past, and if you don't do that, you can't move forward. There is a great deal of embarrassment," she said.

For food detectives trying to reclaim Sephardic cuisine, Inquisition trial records are a valuable resource chronicling dietary practices and exotic ingredients. Among medieval Jews, poultry was often used to break fasts. It was roasted, stewed, fried, and baked into savory pies called empanadas. They were also stuffed with vegetables, cheese, fish, and a wide variety of meats.

Those pastries—and also others inspired by Muslim recipes—are staples in La Taberna de Boabdil's kitchen. Francisco tries to tempt newcomers with sampler dishes, willing people with his infectious enthusiasm and hard resolve. If local diners find him incomprehensible, he targets tourists with a colorful indigo ceramic advertisement for Boabdil on the main street spelled out in English and Spanish. Yet his recipes of ancient tribes have attracted wildly varied reviews.

The critiques, posted online from diners from Rome to Madrid, range from "Most memorable meal in Spain!" to "Worst meal in Spain!" Some complained about dirty tablecloths, a lack of posted prices, the pressure to choose expensive tourist sampler meals, and his homemade rosé wine from his grandmother's recipe.

I knew from experience that Francisco had his good days and bad days when he seemed a little less engaged. He clearly preferred to steer first-time diners to a sampler meal of Andalusian dishes that cost about $15 a person. When pressed for a menu, he offered up a sepia-colored page of dishes with Trufita Sefardi—a truffle of cheese and crushed almonds—at the top of the list of Andalusian cuisine. There were no prices, though, next to any dish.

Yet other diners dismiss the criticism, praising the chef's entertaining and enthusiastic style as part of the restaurant's charm. On one point they all agree: Francisco is a true eccentric. But no one needs a guidebook to figure that out.

"We followed his recommendations for our food choices and were very impressed by them all. He had a story to go with each one," wrote a California diner. "Amazing restaurant; the dirty tablecloths are part of the experience!"

Many locals aren't as open to the experience. Some of our friends went for dinner once, but they found Francisco moody—enthusiastic at times or absentminded, paying more attention to his computer behind the bar counter than to guests. I wasn't sure what to expect when I invited my husband and daughter the first time for a rosy twilight dinner at Boabdil. Francisco steered us to a corner table on the terrace on the edge of the cliff with a view of the valley and clusters of prickly pear cactus ripe with pink fruit. New Age Sephardic music drifted from the cave and a few other diners sat around us, waiting for meals. Sure enough, there were no menus or posted prices, but we took his advice to try the sampler. He scraped a chair to our table and sat with us, turning a meal into a performance in his self-appointed role as *cronista* of cuisine.

"Try this." He pressed us with huge ivory plates crowned with savory pastries. He plucked a meat pastry, Brik Sefardi, stuffed with delicately spiced meat and vegetables. From there we moved on to a dish that he said was inspired by the Moors.

"I call this Dedos de Morayma." He admired a tapa of crab and tomatoes. "It is inspired by a poem about a woman's delicate white fingers." Then we moved on to another appetizer, of cashew nuts, fresh cheese from Ronda, and spinach from the Guadalete valley.

"All of my recipes are not recipes, they are fragments of history. I look for stories of the Andalusians represented in cuisine. There are some people who are painters, who express with paintings. There are singers, who remember history with their voice. And there are cooks, who remember the stories of our past in the kitchen."

To illustrate, he selected a golden *rumaikiya*, a marzipan cake lightly flavored with orange blossoms. "This is the fragrance of Arcos in springtime and Semana Santa," he said.

My husband remained skeptical, though he did strive to bridge the language gap by trying to make polite conversation in his Spanish with a heavy French accent. "How do you make it?" he asked.

He and I were unprepared for the response. But perhaps we should not have been.

Francisco gazed at him, smiling politely and leaning back in his chair.

"That's a secret."

TWELVE

Pruning the Tree

Arcos de la Frontera, 2008

The DNA kit was delivered in a small brown envelope with three little swabs, liquid storage vials, and primitive how-to line drawings with the look of illustrations from a 1950s technical manual. The swabs were used to scrape the inner lining of the cheek to collect cell samples for testing, and they were then packed in the vials for return to a Texas-based testing company, Family Tree DNA.

It had not taken much urging to persuade my father to take the test, though my first e-mail with my strange request was initially ignored. But eventually my father agreed, and I ordered a DNA kit to be sent to him. I also scraped my own samples, but this would give information only about my maternal lines. I asked my father to join me because his DNA sample would reveal his maternal and paternal lines, which might offer clues to track distant relatives and lost branches of the family tree.

The advantage of the testing is that it can tell you if two individual men share a common male ancestor or whether there are connections to others with similar-sounding surnames. The disadvantage is unexpected information: relatives who don't match, hidden adoptions, false paternities—bends in the river of ancestors. The ultimate surprise is if there are no matches—an ancestral black hole of nothingness.

"The DYS markers are short tandem repeats, sequences of DNA that consist of repetitions of a short motif—GATAGATAGATAGATAGATA—and so on. They are found throughout the genome, and they vary from individual to individual in the number of times they are repeated. That's what the numbers in the results are. They mutate quite fast: they can add or subtract one unit once every five hundred father-son transmissions," Francesc Calafell, the Barcelona geneticist, told me.

When my father's results arrived from Family Tree—sent by e-mail from California to Spain—I was baffled by mysterious codes within a series of twelve numbers. His initial test revealed that his haplogroup is a G, which quick research revealed originated in India or Pakistan dispersing to Central Asia, Europe, and the Middle East. Its G2 branch was commonly found in Europe or the Middle East. When I checked

Francesc's study sample of Sephardic Jews, I saw it was dominated by three haplogroups: J1, J2, and my father's type, G.

Some families have used these genetic clues to resolve family mysteries or confirm legends passed down through generations. Descendants of Thomas Jefferson, the third president of the United States, verified stories that they were most likely descendants of Jefferson and his slave Sally Hemings, ultimately through DNA testing in 1998 and 2001 by comparing Y chromosomes. The paternity, which couldn't be established with certainty, showed strong evidence that Jefferson fathered Hemings's children. Further research showed that the Jefferson line was K2—or now a T haplotype. It is rare in Europe, more common in people of the Middle East and Africa. For that reason, researchers believe Jefferson's haplotype descended from migrations of Sephardic Jews in the fifteenth and sixteenth centuries to the New World. This theory is based on some educated guesses from geneticists like Michael Hammer, a researcher at the University of Arizona, who compared Jefferson's chromosome with his database of Y chromosomes and found close matches with four men. There was a perfect match to the Y chromosome of a Moroccan Jew, and matches that differed by two mutations from another Moroccan Jew, a Kurdish Jew, and an Egyptian.

When my father's Y chromosome results arrived, I waited eagerly for similar clues. With the growing collection of DNA samples through companies like Family Tree, I could check online for a potential bounty of distant cousins, with e-mail addresses and home countries included. I monitored this obsessively for a while, but nothing turned up. Every day the computer screen flickered with the same disappointing message: no matches.

In contrast, when I tested my own mitochondrial DNA, genetic material from my mother's side, I received alerts about matches within a few days. These genetic heirlooms are passed down from females to both sons and daughters, but sons do not pass down their mother's DNA to their own children.

In my e-mail box arrived a note from one of those matches, Wilda Obey, an indefatigable amateur genealogy researcher living near Hinckley, Minnesota—the home state of my mother, Carol Ann Roach. Like my mother's family, Wilda's relatives were immigrants from Norway who settled initially in Northfield, Minnesota.

Within days of our exchanging messages with each other, she had identified a shared ancestor of my great-grandmother Uni Urevig. She also linked the same ancestor to another man, who had the exact five mutations on her haplogroup. Meanwhile, my computer account with Family Tree continued to send out the same message for my father's haplotype of G: no matches.

I decided to call Bennett Greenspan, the president of Family Tree DNA, who fires off e-mails with the company motto, "History Unearthed Daily," from the company's headquarters in Houston. Enthusiastic and chatty, he plays an outsize role as the company's ardent top salesman, appearing on television news shows and radio programs to extol in his folksy manner the value of hunting for ancestors.

My problem, I told him, was that my family gene pool seemed empty. Not one person had come close to my father's DNA signature of a series of twelve numbers.

"Right now, I just can't tell you if the Carvajals were Jews because I just don't have enough information," Bennett said. "Clearly your father is not matching anyone."

"What does that signify?"

"The typical distribution of DNA looks like this. You have a few exact matches in a series of numbers. You have a few that are off by one number. Then you have matches that are off by more numbers. The further you go out, the more you allow for a deviation and the more people you pick up.

"Quite often Jewish DNA signatures don't look that way. Generally you have a couple of matches. You have no matches at all. What it means is that you're isolated on the branch of the tree of mankind. And we have to ask why."

Together with the International Institute for Jewish Genealogy, Greenspan and researchers at universities in Israel, New York, and Arizona are using DNA samples for a Sephardic migration study that traces the origins of conversos who fled Spain for the former Ottoman Empire, Italy, and Greece.

Haplogroup G, he told me, is found in some villages of northern Portugal, ten miles from the Spanish border, in as much as nineteen percent of the population. He said it may reflect migration of Sephardic Jews during the Inquisition, who fled Spain across the border to escape persecution. But he found my father's codes puzzling, even after he rechecked them with his database.

"The most important matches are your exact matches. The next important standard is a series with one mismatch in the sequence. Then two-step mismatches. Your father has no matches at all." Greenspan seemed as disappointed by this realization as I was.

"We have to do a little more testing to understand why. That unusual distribution is more likely from the Black Plague because Jews died in greater percentages, and the surviving non-Jews did their best to kill them. This is what we call a bottleneck or a crash that tends to leave the family tree looking odd.

"I'm not seeing any match at all to your father's twelve-marker set. It means that the family tree has been pruned with a hatchet."

He said that to me as if I should understand what he meant. So I felt a little dense asking the same basic question.

"I'm sorry, I don't understand 'pruning the tree.' What do you mean?"

"Lots of your ancestors were killed."

THIRTEEN

There Is a Season

Arcos de la Frontera, 2008

Don Manuel relished hunting down secrets and he savored each triumph like slaying a giant. He believed that a writer is a man who bleeds from his pen and so he was unafraid to confront the powerful.

Maybe his rebellious streak was the result of the blood coursing in his veins, the legacy of a distant relative, José Ulloa, El Tragabuches. In a museum in Ronda, there are paintings of the eighteenth-century bullfighter turned *bandolero* and smuggler whose hideout was in the Sierra Morena. Don Manuel corrected people who referred to his ancestor as a *bandido*. Don Manuel argued that there was a vast difference between a *bandido*—"an individual delinquent"—and an

Andalusian *bandolero*, a Spanish Robin Hood who aided the poor from miserable villages and clashed with local tyrants.

El Tragabuches, born in Arcos de la Frontera, famously turned to the life of a *bandolero* after returning home to find his girlfriend, La Nena, with the local church sexton. He blamed his life of crime on her betrayal, and artists would later paint his pain with watercolors in early comic-book style: El Tragabuches discovers his girlfriend's hidden lover, slays him, and throws her out of a second-story window of a little white house.

As the town *cronista*, Don Manuel targeted one of the pueblo's aristocratic families, the Marqueses de Torresoto, who have now vanished from the life of Arcos, ruined by financing the nineteenth-century Carlist war to support a pretender to the Spanish throne.

Don Manuel tracked down the contents of a mysterious message in an eighteenth-century *relicario*, a reliquary of Santo Cristo del Romeral that was kept in the church of San Pedro. It was donated by a nun who was the daughter of one Marqués de Torresoto, a notorious womanizer. Through the centuries, new pastors at San Pedro were instructed never to give out the key to the *relicario*. Inside was the nun's blunt confession: "God in his infinite goodness, have mercy on the father of all of us seven children because he is a very great sinner."

The *cronista*'s biggest find was his investigation of rebels who participated in the shadowy network of the Spanish Maquis, left-wing guerrillas and antifascists exiled in France in the 1930s after the Spanish Civil War. They taught vital skills to the French during World War II. They sabotaged roads, staged robberies, fashioned bombs, and assassinated Francoists and Nazis. Resistance was their natural state. Franco's secretive government declared victory over the movement that continued after the war, jailing and executing hundreds of guerrillas, whose heroism in France was largely forgotten. But the *cronista* dug deep and discovered a curious fact about the wily Maquis: In reality, many of the old veterans who fought the Guardia Civil in Spain survived years after Franco's death and lived in leisurely retirement in Andalusia.

A rebellious Don Manuel would periodically challenge authorities in an effort to protect his beloved hometown. One ongoing battle involved Santiago de Mora-Figueroa y Williams, the Marqués of Tamarón and a former Spanish ambassador to England, whose family owns a Moorish fortress that looms over the summit of Arcos.

The landmark was built before the eleventh century for the Taifa kingdom of the Jazrun dynasty. But this historical jewel's imposing wooden doors are resolutely closed to the public by the owner, a descendant of a wealthy British couple who purchased and restored the castle and lived there through the 1950s. Don Manuel, naturally, pushed for the opening of the landmark with a singular lack of success.

After the town's annual August fiesta celebrating its patron saint, Don Manuel turned his sights on Father Domingo to take on a new crusade. He was the austere pastor of the

Basilica of Santa María, and was politely known among church members for his dry manner. Perhaps Don Manuel was harsher on the priest because he was naturally suspicious, well aware of the town's history of local curates who managed to enrich themselves at the church's expense.

For three centuries Don Manuel's Pérez ancestors were Santa María's caretakers, who all carried the grand title of *maestro de fábrica*, master of production. His uncle, Rafael, was the last to hold the position that had been held in the family since 1693. The job vanished when he died in 1990, but Don Manuel seemed to inherit an innate sense of responsibility for the church. In one black-and-white photograph, from the 1970s or 1980s, he is dressed in a suit, arms folded, preparing to take inventory of the church's treasures with the previous pastor.

Don Manuel's tensions with the priest, Father Domingo, began with the mysterious disappearance of a four-hundred-year-old gold medallion, engraved with a portrait of Mary and baby Jesus cradled in her left arm. The medal, encrusted with sixty-one emeralds, sparkled around the neck of one of the town's most important images, La Virgen del Rosario, every August when the Brotherhood of Vera Cruz paraded her with roses at her dainty porcelain feet.

Local jewelers had long marveled at the quality of the jewels, which they considered an authentic museum piece valued at millions of euros. There was no signature or mark on the medallion, but it appeared to have been crafted somewhere in South America, perhaps Peru or Ecuador, a gift to

Santa María by one of the many returning explorers from the New World.

Between 1523 and 1789, many men from Arcos traveled on expeditions to the Western Hemisphere. Andalusia grew rich in the spoils of the New World, but when the seafaring economy crashed, they had no alternative industries and the south became the poorest region of Spain. Don Manuel believed that this glittering emerald medallion was commissioned by an eighteenth-century explorer, Miguel Antonio Calderón de la Torre, who had returned from Peru with a bounty of gold and stones.

One August, at the height of summer vacation, brotherhood members went to retrieve the medallion in a special locked room where Santa María stored its treasures. They were stunned to find it had gone missing while Santa María was closed to the public for two years of renovation. The second-story room was locked and accessible to only a few people within the church. But Santa María's alarm system for its museum treasures, paid for by the local city hall, was disconnected at a time that hundreds of people were milling in the plaza below on a feast day. Two windows, however, were open permanently for ventilation, making it possible for someone with a sophisticated ladder to break in during the early-morning hours.

After the robbery, the local newspaper, *Arcos Información*, cited Guardia Civil sources who said that Father Domingo had forbidden anyone to call the police on the Sunday that the theft was discovered until he knew more about what had happened the Friday before. Later he also refused to comment until he had permission from his bishop, provoking furious speculation about whether the mysterious disappearance was truly a theft. It had all the classic hallmarks of an inside job, and worse, according to Alvaro Troncoso, a friend of Don Manuel, the parish priest pressed Don Manuel not to write about it. But he refused, lodging a complaint with the Guardia Civil about the robbery because it was his suspicion that the emerald had been sold abroad.

Then Don Manuel went public with his suspicions in an opinion piece in the *Arcos Información*. To his friends and family, Don Manuel complained bitterly that the disappearance of the medallion was not actually a theft but a discreet transfer of church property without the permission of the pueblo.

"The Church has never permitted photographs and they have not declared anything," Don Manuel wrote in a special opinion piece in the local weekly, a few days after the robbery was revealed. "Maybe they are hoping that it will not be noticed or will be ignored and forgotten by the people of Arcos de la Frontera. They have talked in the press about the responsibilities of the Church, but here there is no equality."

Other officials from the parish of San Francisco issued a letter in support of Santa María, praising the pastor as a top fund-raiser for the church. Eventually, the outcry and suspicions faded away like the hum notes of Santa María's bells on a still afternoon.

"There are some people who feel the pain of a pueblo,"

Don Manuel's wife, Mari, told me once while discussing his character. "Manolo felt the pain of Arcos more than his family, more than his children, more than his house."

Several months later, I put in a request to view a record from Santa María's archives. That's when I met Father Domingo, at the church office, which was on a side street across from Santa María. Father Domingo would not allow me to touch the aging leather *legajo* filled with sepia-colored baptismal records dating back to the eighteenth century. He sat across from me at a wooden table and read the information aloud in a sonorous voice. My daughter, Claire, sat at my side, listening in silence.

I was looking for baptismal records, although I wasn't sure what they would show me. I had requested in particular the documents for Pedro Acosta, a converso born in 1630 who was tried twice by inquisitors for "Judaizing" and whose property, down the hill from where we lived, was confiscated. I was curious to know more about the man whose white house near the church of San Francisco was still universally known as the House of Anguish, or Casa de Angustias.

Father Domingo could not find any records from the 1600s, but he did locate a 1737 document for the baptism of the son of Catalina Acosta, which he read to me, noting that the name was rare. When he referred to the presiding priest at the baptism as a *calificador* of the Holy Office of the Inquisition, I interrupted him to ask about the title. I knew that these Inquisition officials were commonly priests who examined preliminary evidence against secretly practicing Jews to decide whether an arrest was warranted.

But Father Domingo ignored my interruption, continuing to read the number and code for the *legajo*. It was clear that I had to wait till he was done.

Once he finished, I posed the question again.

"Was this a baptism of a converso, since the priest was connected to the Inquisition?"

"Oh, no." He shook his head. "It was just a title for the priest."

I was not convinced, but I knew that there was no arguing with that logic. So I changed topics. I turned to the mystery of the missing gold medallion of La Virgen del Rosario that was stolen from the church of Santa María, to the dismay of Don Manuel.

"I've read a lot about the history of religious art here and I wondered if the medallion was ever recovered."

"The police are investigating, and there is no news."

"How much was it worth?"

"I don't know. They say millions."

"How is this possible that this could have happened?"

"I don't know. Nobody knows."

I nodded. It was obvious that La Virgen del Rosario would never again sway through the streets of Arcos wearing her emeralds and gold.

When we left the dark wood church office to walk below the bright blue sky of Arcos toward the Guadalete River, my daughter finally delivered her observations.

"It's like the closet in Narnia," she said, referring to the C. S. Lewis novel about children entering a fantasy world through the doors of a wood armoire. "And now we are leaving the prison."

⊃⋅⊂

Don Manuel was not the only rebel in the pueblo.

One summer a sand-colored sculpture appeared on the main street of Calle de la Corredera, the most ancient road in Arcos. The sculpture was installed by the Socialist city government to promote the pueblo's landmark tourist draw, Semana Santa. Three robed and hooded figures, images of brotherhood penitents, loomed over the bustling commercial area. One grasped an iron lantern and another a lattice cross. Behind them stood an even more enormous crucifix.

Some local merchants grumbled privately that the primitive images looked sinister, but they kept the criticism to themselves. As people grew accustomed to the hoods in their daily midst, someone dressed them up like giant dolls in blue-and-white robes of the San Antonio brotherhood on tourism day.

Then one night, thieves wrenched the lattice cross from the main statue. Without this powerful symbol, the robed figure that once held it looked like a hooded boxer with fists poised to punch the air.

The neighborhood association president, Felipe Iglesias Medina, expressed outrage, calling the disappearance of the

cross an act of "idiots and vandals" seeking to cause maxi-
mum damage to Christians who make up "the majority of
the pueblo."

"Justice," he thundered in the local newspaper, "will be
done."

When I heard the cross had been stolen, my first reaction
was to call Don Manuel. Flashes like that come and go, and
then I remembered with sadness that it was impossible.

In March 2008, still weeks before the arrival of Easter, I
was in France, preparing to head for Arcos. I had a letter in an
envelope for Don Manuel, seeking to meet him for advice
about excavating my family history. My notes and folders
were collected by my desk. I had studied all four densely written volumes in Spanish of his *History of Arcos de la Frontera
Through Its Streets*, from Abades to Zorilla. I had highlighted
his own brief passage about himself in reference to a dead-
end street on the western side of Arcos that was named Calle
de Manuel Pérez Regordán in April 1990. It was a relatively
new street, with a Yoigo mobile telephone store, a Canrol
auto shop, and an herbalist's, offering health and diet remedies. The city made sure that it had not erased a historical
name when it posted Don Manuel's.

Ever the historian, he took note of all the buildings on the
street, adding a short history of himself. He listed his books
and ongoing investigations and a tribute from a longtime
friend, who recalled a fabled bullfight they watched together
in Jerez with Antonio Ordóñez, a leading bullfighter in the

1950s and one of the dueling matadors chronicled by Ernest Hemingway in *The Dangerous Summer.* "Why do I recall this? Because, with your intelligence and tenacity, enormous dedication and effort, you have labored for future generations and therefore you deserve a bullfighter's ultimate prize: two ears and a tail. You will be a landmark, a reference in the history of histories of Arcos."

I read that reference and made a mental note to ask Don Manuel about how he felt being viewed as a landmark the next time I saw him in person in Arcos. With the *cronista*, I always encountered a polite reserve. But through the pages of his books, I considered him a literary friend. He was a fellow hunter tracking our quarry: the past and its lessons.

So it was that one morning I checked the online version of the pueblo's *Arcos Información*, the weekly newspaper, which covers the twists of the local political parties and displays photos of area farmers showing off enormous pumpkins or the latest triumph of a flamenco champion.

I was stunned to glimpse Don Manuel's name in a headline. The *cronista*, who was currently pursuing an investigation of the Inquisition in the province of Cádiz, had added his own Gothic chapter of personal tragedy to the history of the town.

In February, after ferrying his gravely ill son, José María, to the hospital, where he was resuscitated three times, Don Manuel himself suffered a thrombosis or blood clot and was rushed to San Rafael Hospital in Cádiz for emergency care.

During weeks of treatment, he suffered another clot, and he started preparing for his death with the same orderly organization that he gave to his vast library. He told his wife of more than fifty years, Mari, that he wanted his funeral at San Pedro, shunning Santa María, which in any case was closed for renovation.

"You are not going to die," snapped Mari, a birdlike woman with clipped silver hair and eyes magnified by thick glasses. "You are getting better, *gracias a Dios*. You have all your faculties. You have so much to finish."

He gazed back at her and grasped her hand. He did not reply, but his sixty-eight-year-old eyes indicated that he knew better.

Several weeks later, he was dead.

With Don Manuel's passing, the pueblo gave the *cronista* his due. Arcos lowered its flags to half-mast and the mayor and assorted local dignitaries turned out for a viewing along with hundreds of Don Manuel's friends. The viewing was fittingly held below the stars in the old synagogue of Misericordia, where Don Manuel had zealously guarded the history that others wanted to forget. His coffin was wrapped with the pueblo's local flag.

For his funeral, Dolores, the *campanera*, tolled the bells at the church of San Pedro, a better refuge to bid good-bye to Don Manuel, given his prickly questions about the disappearance of the missing gold medallion from the Basilica of Santa María.

Some of the mourners were left wondering if anyone

could carry on Don Manuel's work. "It hurts me a lot that there is no one after him to worry about our history," said Francisco Saborido, who recalled that Don Manuel planned to write about how his cave restaurant had been a clandestine synagogue for Jewish conversos.

Now I could only wonder what Don Manuel would think about new mysteries: the town's missing cross and my own family's secrets.

Unfortunately, he was not there to chronicle his own family drama, which was impossible to ignore during his funeral mass. His three children were all there, including a second son, Jacinto, a prisoner in a jail 150 miles away in Huelva. He entered through a side chapel with two local policemen. His hair was tied tightly in a braid, and suit sleeves discreetly covered his handcuffs. Mari, the widow, was inwardly seething at the mayor for refusing her request to remove the cuffs. In front of all of the mourners, she rose from her seat at the front of the pews and warmly embraced her errant son.

My friends who were there watched and thought how in Andalusia, there was a thin veneer under which everything seemed to be functioning, but actually everything was breaking down.

At the end of Don Manuel's funeral, the bells of San Pedro tolled wildly for a man who could not bear to abandon the seventy-seven *calles* of the old quarter. The *campanera*, Dolores, tugged the ropes, choosing a combination from a repertoire of four forms for funerals, *entierro general*.

"Streets, streets of Arcos, open to the four winds," Don Manuel once wrote. "Streets to hear sonorous bronze bells from the towers of Santa María and San Pedro. These are my streets, my beloved streets of Arcos."

The truth is that his death hit me much harder than I had expected. I had lost a literary friend who never knew how much his inspiration and dogged digging and stubbornness meant to me. I had planned to enlist Don Manuel as my guide and mentor when I settled in Arcos de la Frontera. When he died, I considered dropping my project, thinking it would be impossible to find direction without the aid of his long experience. But I shared his love for the pueblo's rich history and decided to continue. I would seek his counsel from his books and magnificent personal library.

His widow readily invited me into his old retreat on Calle de Juan del Valle. Scholars came occasionally to study in his archives and so she was not surprised when I came calling after his death. I filled out a special visitor's card before settling at a long marble table with some of the books that Don Manuel had carefully collected over the course of sixty years. The library gave me a sense of peace. I liked the smell of old paper and pristine leather covers. I liked leafing through his folders of loose documents, typed in Times New Roman.

As I touched the cold marble of his writing table, I tried to feel traces of the old *cronista*. Once again, I faced the same situation I had faced with my own grandmother Mamita. It was too late to pose unanswered questions.

After my first library visit, Mari invited me into her living room that also doubled as a sewing room. I huddled next to a small wooden table where she wove ivory lace with dozens of spools of thread, a skill she learned as a girl from Belgian nuns at convent school.

Dolores, the *campanera*, was also visiting, but she didn't say much and she left soon after, since it was nearly time to ring the noon bells.

"It's a beautiful house," I said, looking around the room, hung with old family pictures.

"It's too much of a house."

"How are you doing? I am so sorry for your loss."

"I feel just regular."

As it turned out, Mari was an unexpected wealth of general and obscure information, from the language of the bells to the proper way to sew pointed green hoods to march in a Semana Santa procession.

After my frequent visits to Don Manuel's library, we would settle in the living room or her kitchen, where tomatoes for gazpacho were simmering on the stove. At lunch she taught me about the *solano*, the wind from the southeast that courses through the summit of Plaza del Cabildo. There was something uneasy in the air when the hot blast arrived from the African desert in the summer. The suffocating currents steamed through the passageways and narrow lanes, dusting white houses with fine Sahara sand. When the *solano* comes, according to a Spanish proverb, it is not time to ask for favors.

The humid air, blue with vapors, made everyone anxious. Birds flew at lower levels. Dogs hid. Horses staggered. The gusts made people melancholy with headaches, insomnia, and dizziness. Andalusians describe someone with the resulting psychological condition as *asolanao.* "It's *el solano* that makes us all crazy," a character explains in *Volver,* a film by director Pedro Almodóvar. Don Manuel knew its power well. Before he died, he asked his wife to scatter his ashes from the brink of Peña Nueva to the lion-colored rocks below. But he issued explicit instructions to carry out the task on a tranquil day. He worried that the dust would blow back into his beloved pueblo, Mari told me.

One day when I visited her, she started bustling in her kitchen and retrieving from the shelves dark bottles of vinegar. I watched her lay down several teaspoons. Then she began a quirky course in vinegar appreciation. Samples of the best sherry vinegars from Jerez de la Frontera lined her kitchen counter, including her particular favorite, Gran Reserva 25. It was aged in oak barrels, as expensive as a bottle of wine. She swirled the burgundy-colored liquids with a silver teaspoon and taught me to appreciate the aroma and complexity of bitterness.

She had long endured it in her own life. It was after we sampled the vinegars that conversation drifted to her wayward son, Jacinto. She and Don Manuel had long been fighting for the early release of their son from prison in Huelva, where he was serving out a sentence of more than thirteen years. But he had compounded his problems by sending an angry letter to a judge about his prison conditions that earned him more jail time for making a personal threat.

"It was the wind that spread the fire to other cars," she said by way of explanation about the blaze that landed her son in jail for a long term. "He didn't hurt anybody."

El solano, I thought.

Her eyes brimmed with tears and she kneaded a tissue as she told me the story. In 1999, Jacinto set fire to his ex-mother-in-law's parked car in Arcos de la Frontera after a breakup with his common-law wife. He had gone to the house of his ex-mother-in-law to recover some belongings, according to his family, but they had been thrown out the window to the street. Don Manuel and Mari had long argued that no one was injured in the fire, which spread to three other cars. Jacinto, Mari told me, suffered from a personality disorder provoked by a drug addiction, and he had made great strides in prison to rehabilitate himself, learning to restore antique furniture.

She was preparing to head to the prison in Huelva to make another appeal for his release, the latest in an ongoing series of petitions organized by the family.

"You could help by writing about it." She dabbed her tears with a crumpled tissue.

"I'm not sure what I can do, but let me think about it."

I left the home of the *cronista* that afternoon, musing about the strange irony of my visit. I had laid plans to seek out

Don Manuel in Arcos, so that he might help me understand converso Jews who escaped the fate of burning at the stake by guarding their secret faith until they lost it through the generations.

Now I was asked to aid his son, who had ignited a fire on Arcos with the help of a malignant wind.

FOURTEEN

El Call

Barcelona, 2010

Synagogues may vanish in Spain, but they are never completely silenced. Their story lives on in their stones.

In the port city of Barcelona, it was nearly six hundred years before a researcher tracked the remains of the ancient Sinagoga Mayor de Barcelona, probably the oldest synagogue in Spain and Europe, dating back to the third or fourth century.

When the dark stone synagogue was finally located, it had transformed into a dry cleaner's and a junk storage site for an electrical supply store through the early 1990s. I learned this when I first walked by the synagogue along a passageway of shadows, Carrer de Marlet. Sheer serendipity had brought me to this quarter of the city to meet with a rabbi who had traveled here from Israel to work with descendants of converso Jews in Spain and Portugal.

I met Rabbi Nissan Ben Avraham for the first time in a freshly painted bookstore, which had opened just a few months earlier in the old Jewish quarter. He was wearing side curls and a yarmulke, a tranquil air of bemusement in his brown eyes. I made a gaffe by extending my hand in introduction to this Orthodox Spanish rabbi, who deftly ignored it. A woman tending the wine shop corrected me, discreetly shaking her head, to instantly teach me the rule that in the Orthodox religion men and women do not touch in public.

He had suggested meeting in the quarter, where the old synagogue had effectively vanished until historian Jaume Riera Sans rediscovered it in 1987. He found it by tracing a thirteenth-century tax collector's route to the subterranean synagogue. The old map, found in the archives of the cathedral of Barcelona, spelled out in precise detail eighty-seven buildings and names of property owners in Barcelona's Jewish quarter.

The telltale clue was the synagogue's unusual alignment. Neighboring buildings faced northwest and southwest, but the synagogue broke that pattern, facing east toward Jerusalem. The cellarlike rooms of a fourteenth-century synagogue had been built atop the remains of an older synagogue. Below was an underground spring for *mikvehs*, ritual baths.

Not until 2002 was the synagogue restored. It was reopened as a museum, a remnant of Barcelona's Jewish quarter, known as El Call, pronounced "el kye." In the local dialect it means "narrow street," for *callejón*, or possibly "community," for the Hebrew word *kahal*. Barcelona's Call reached its zenith in the twelfth and thirteenth centuries, when it emerged as a center of Jewish learning in medieval Europe with a school of mysticism known as Kabbalah.

Within El Call, the Jewish courtier class dominated public service as physicians, administrators, and tax collectors. The families of Benveniste, Eleazar, and Sheshet struck close relationships with the Spanish court, advising kings, bailiffs, and property owners. But these positions of power placed Jews in a precarious position when power shifted. In the popular imagination of the time, Jewish officials were linked with royalty and privilege. Constant warfare increased the burden of taxes, which were often collected by Jews in the service of kings. Antimonarchical sentiment easily turned on Jews.

For the common people and their Christian pastors, the popular image of Jews became something diabolical to be invoked in Sunday sermons. In the early fourteenth century, the popular view spread across Europe that Jews were poisoners, in league with lepers, and desecrators of Communion hosts. They were also accused of kidnapping and murdering Christian children at Easter, a myth that some clergy spread with support from Alfonso X, the thirteenth-century king of

Castile, who claimed, "We have heard it said that in certain places on Good Friday the Jews steal children and set them on the cross in a mocking manner."

This toxic mood intensified after a mysterious plague struck Europe in 1348. No one knew the source of the Black Plague or what caused it. The deadly disease appeared with swellings and blackened the skin with gangrene. Death was swift, coming in two to seven days. The plague ravaged Europe, killing by some estimates some 75 million people—a third of Europe's population—between 1347 and 1351.

Fear transformed into murderous frenzy, whipped by a Dominican archdeacon in Seville named Ferrand Martinez, who himself was descended from Jewish conversos. The Black Plague struck with particular virulence in the close quarters of the Jewish Call, turning Jews into the scapegoats for the source of the plague. In 1378, Martinez proposed his solution to the "Jewish problem": destruction of Seville's twenty-three synagogues.

With the deaths of the king of Castile and the archbishop in 1390, Martinez's power was unchecked; he became de facto ruler of the region. He intensified his campaign against the Jews, seizing advantage of a power vacuum to stir a mob of followers who entered the *calls* in different cities, flagellating themselves with chains as proof of their Christian faith.

On June 4, 1391, a mob burned down the gates of the Jewish quarter in Barcelona and killed Jews who refused to convert to Christianity on the spot. The pogroms spread across Spain to the Balearic Islands and Majorca, where the governor brought the local Jews to a fortress to protect them. But the crowds broke through and delivered an ultimatum: Convert or die.

In Barcelona, more than four hundred Jews were killed on August 10 of that year. Rioters targeted tax collectors and attacked the synagogue, which was not only a center for prayer and worship but also a symbol of law in the community. Practically all the Aragonese Jewish quarters were destroyed in bloody rioting, with the mob bent on burning their debts. But the key to quelling the riots was conversion. Only in Zaragoza—where the king of Aragon lived and exerted control—were the Jews spared.

By the time the riots sputtered out after a year, estimates are that 100,000 Jews converted, another 100,000 were killed, and 100,000 more fled to Muslim lands in the Ottoman Empire.

The next major exodus came a century later, when Queen Isabella I of Castile and King Ferdinand II of Aragon issued the Edict of Expulsion. Jews had four months to settle their businesses and leave the country and they were not permitted to take any gold or silver with them. For that reason, many historians believe that King Ferdinand, who was the model for Machiavelli's *The Prince*, had developed a plot to erase his enormous war debts. He had just fought a war to oust the last Moorish ruler of Granada. The war, financed in part with loans from Jews, ended in triumph in early 1492. After the victory, King Ferdinand withdrew his protection of Jews, issuing the edict that allowed the kingdom's debts to vanish and gave it the right to confiscate the properties and fortunes of exiled Jews.

Writers from that time recounted the exodus in Barcelona, with thousands of Jews lining up to board ships bound for refuges in North Africa and Turkey in the Ottoman Empire. Some fled to Portugal, but that was temporary as well: Jews were later expelled from there in 1496. On July 31, 1492, the last Jew left Spain. Yet they by no means disappeared.

Today some Hebrew inscriptions are still visible on stones taken from an old Jewish cemetery on Montjuïc, a hill in Barcelona. They are embedded in the façade of Lloctinent Palace, which was built in the fourteenth century near the Jewish quarter as a residence for nobles and used two centuries later by Inquisition officials.

In the past few years, there have been faint signals of revival in El Call. Near the synagogue, there is a newly opened shop, Call Barcelona Wine & Books, that is affiliated with the local Chabad Lubavitch center.

Yet the mood of unease never completely vanished. In January 2009—as fighting erupted again in the Gaza Strip—a man smashed a baseball bat against the ancient synagogue and then attacked an employee who approached him. The same month, the windows of Barcelona's Chabad House were shattered by vandals and the building was sprayed with anti-Semitic graffiti and the word ASSASSINS.

I didn't know what to expect when Rabbi Nissan Ben Avraham agreed to meet me in El Call. If anyone could translate painful history into modern present, it was Rabbi Avraham. By age fifty-two, he had come to terms with a dual identity: a Catholic schoolboy from the Spanish island of Mallorca who broke with his family to reclaim the ancient Jewish roots of his father's converso family.

We took wooden seats at the back of the bookstore, the piped Sephardic music sometimes overwhelming his low voice. He is the emissary for Shavei Israel, a Jerusalem-based group that offers religious training for converso descendants from Spain and Portugal. And he was waiting in the bookstore for one of his students, a young Spanish man who had yearned to become a priest but then learned that his family had been maintaining Jewish rituals.

The rabbi was born Nicolau Aguiló, the eldest of seven children and the son of a Christian mother and a merchant descended from conversos. The family still has the ancient property records of their haberdashery shop, dating to 1686, when ancestors purchased it from Inquisition officials. That suggests, according to the rabbi, that the store was confiscated, and then repurchased by the family after some ancestors were tried in 1677 and issued light penalties.

Nicolau went to mass every week, but, he remembered, he was still taunted on the school playground as a *chueta*, or *xueta* in Catalan. On the island, that was the term for converso descendants, a name that may have referred to salted pork—for the meat the converts ate to demonstrate their sincere conversion to Christianity.

An old friend from my university days in Berkeley

recalled a children's rhyme he learned while growing up on the island of Mallorca that mocked each of the converso families: *"Picó picaba, Miró miraba . . ."* They learned early on to be suspicious of about fifteen converso families, among them one with the rabbi's own surname, Aguiló, and Bonnín, Cortés, Forteza, Fuster, Martí, Miró, Picó, Piña, Pomar, Segura, Tarongí, Valentí, Valleriola, and Valls. Inquisitors focused on the conversos who lived in the former Jewish port of call of Mallorca, where many merchants inherited their occupations. Most of the jewelry shops in Mallorca's silver district are still run today by *chuetas*.

Some people paid or struck deals to have their names removed, among them a family called Moya. That is the family name of my great-grandmother Anaïs Moya, the daughter of a doctor, Santiago, who moved his family from Cuba to Colombia to Costa Rica.

The persecution of *chuetas* also dates back to the summer of 1391, when riots in Seville spread to Mallorca and unleashed hostility that endured for centuries. Priests who were the descendants of *chuetas* were not allowed to say mass in the island's cathedral until the 1960s. Polls taken as late as 2001 by the Universitat de les Illes Balears show that thirty percent of Mallorcans declared that they would not marry a *chueta*, and a small aging minority of five percent said they would not even accept them as friends.

By the mid–twentieth century, the distrust had faded—or at least been blunted—and Mallorca became more of a tourist destination and open to outsiders. Still, some popular

Spanish expressions reflect deep-seated hostility toward Jews: *"No te fíes del judío converso, ni su hijo, ni de su nieto."* Never trust a Jewish converso, nor his son, nor his grandson. To this day, the church of Saint Eulalia, which drew a number of descendants of conversos to its parish, is casually called Sinagoga de Santa Eulalia.

Rabbi Ben Avraham remembers a pivotal moment in his own spiritual life when he was about ten years old. He drove with his mother down Carrer de Jafudà Cresques. The street was named after a fabled Jewish cartographer who was forced to convert; Cresques developed the Catalan Atlas, which showed the world's navigational routes in six panels. When little Nicolau pointed to the street sign, he blurted out: *"¡Chueta!"*

"Why are you laughing?" he recalls his mother saying. "You, too, are a *chueta*."

Unsettled by his mother's response, Nicolau approached his father with questions. "In the house we were all Catholic, but in school the other students said I was Jewish. At first, my father didn't want to say anything about this. But it interested me because of the significance that after hundreds of years they continued to mark these families, describing them as Jews, even though they were all going to mass."

Some people encouraged his interest, while his own father dismissed his efforts as reaching back to dead history, according to the rabbi. In his house the silence on the subject was absolute. "This fact was never mentioned, and we never behaved according to any Jewish custom," he said. "I wanted to cease fleeing, to free myself from the Jewish sign that the Inquisition placed upon the Jewish converts."

He paused for a moment and we listened to drifts of Sephardic music as we sat in the bookshop on two straight-backed chairs.

"I am the only one to make the way back. The main problem was that my father thought that going back to Judaism is like going back two thousand years. He was a good Christian and didn't understand what's wrong with the Christian message."

Eventually, the rabbi studied in Israel and officially converted, married a Jewish woman, and raised twelve children. The strains between him and his father eventually eased.

"When he came to see his first grandson, the way to reconciliation was easier," he said.

Other descendants have made brutal choices after discovering their origins, he said. "They break with all of the past. But I believe it is a psychological stage to be able to grow and develop a new identity. It is like an adolescent who needs to escape—to demonstrate 'I am a different person. I am not a copy of my father.' Much later, when they mature, they can understand that they can mend relations."

As a teacher, he offers guidance to about forty converso descendants scattered among Barcelona, Valencia, Mallorca, and Seville. It is a journey that he says can take as long as thirty years because "it's very difficult, a long process of exploration. They can't decide whether to continue or to identify themselves with a new religion. They don't know what to do."

Along with Rabbi Ben Avraham, other rabbis have been dispatched by the same Jerusalem organization across Europe, offering lessons and counseling to descendants of Jews in Poland who hid their religious roots during World War II and to lost tribes of Jews from India, Brazil, and China.

"This is very fashionable," Rabbi Ben Avraham said of the Spanish descendants' seeking to reclaim their religious roots. "There are many folkloric stories. My grandmother told my mother, who told me. These are things that are very difficult to prove."

There is also a deep historical reluctance in Judaism to welcome back descendants despite the Jewish community's concern over their decreasing numbers. It is a fear with roots in the Middle Ages when Jews were accused of "stealing Christians" and they were a minority religion living under restrictions that barred Jewish missionaries.

It also reflects conservative anxiety over what constitutes a Jew. In modern-day Israel, conversos from Spain may seek to convert to the religion of their ancestors, but they are not instantly recognized as Jews because of their historical family background.

The rabbi and other supporters have been discreetly pressing for this recognition. He has been lobbying a prominent private rabbinical court in Israel to study in particular the *chuetas* of Mallorca because the converso families remained on the island, married among themselves, and are closely intertwined with elaborate family trees.

"How did you choose an identity?" I asked Rabbi Ben Avraham. "What if you don't have clear proof of being a Jew, just bits of clues?"

"Little by little, distance grows with the past or an angle of the past," he said. "Then comes a moment when you say, 'I have nothing to do with this.' There is a magic moment when you say, 'That's it, I am a Jew,' in a loud, strong voice."

The rabbi's voice was actually almost a whisper as he offered this advice, and I strained to hear him as he spoke in Spanish. People passed by us in our two rigid chairs, as they browsed books of Jewish history that lined the shelves of the shop.

His words chilled me, a fleeting shiver. As a reporter, I am accustomed to suppressing feelings, a habit that seems to have pervaded my life. I didn't know how to release this emotion. I bade the rabbi good-bye and left the bookshop, wandering out to the dark alleys of Barcelona's old Jewish quarter.

Is this the moment? I wondered.

FIFTEEN

Saving Voice

Arcos de la Frontera, 2008

In a cramped corner bakery near Calle del Guadalete, Mari Camarena presided over fragrant racks of warm *bolillo* loaves with the regal bearing of a flour-dusted queen in a white coat.

The baker has the same proud bearing during flamenco shows at her unmarked club, which is grandly known as Peña Flamenca Femenina Mari Camarena. Entrance is by invitation only. Her club is crowded with family-style tables and a small stage in the cellar of her sprawling two-story brick house. The *peña* is a secluded place off a country road on the outskirts of Arcos where the night is so blue-black that the only way to find it is to drive along the road and listen hard for a guitar thrum or wait for the flash of car headlights turning right toward a dirt field next to her house.

I had searched a long time for an intimate *peña* like this with flamenco music sung from the soul. For tourists, there are bland dinner shows in Jerez de la Frontera that cater to customers who come for local sherry bodega tours. I've overheard the women in the tourist office at the summit of Arcos de la Frontera advising visitors to head there for the three-course dinners at clubs in Barrio Santiago, the heart of Jerez's old Gypsy quarter.

The first time I visited Mari Camarena's club, we were summoned by an invitation on a torn scrap of paper jotted with her address and phone number. Mari's silver-haired husband, Pedro Carrera, delivered it by hand to my neighbor, María José, across the lane. She then passed it to me. I was never quite sure how he found my street or why I was invited, but it's further proof that no one can hide in this pueblo. I found out later that Manuel Zapata, the son of the fabled *saeta* singer Zapata, asked for the invitation from Mari, who is a second-generation *saeta* singer.

When my husband and I arrived at the club, I saw a man with a gray ponytail peeking out of his felt fedora, leaning against a wall. He introduced himself as Señor Flores, patriarch of a local Gypsy clan of flamenco singers from Arcos. Two of his sons are professional performers and teachers, working in Jerez de la Frontera, Madrid, and Seville. He himself sings, and sometimes his granddaughters dance beside him at small gatherings.

"Are we too late? Has it already started?" I asked Señor Flores, who is wise in the ways of *peña* rituals.

"The music?" he said with a wry grin. "You're obviously not from around here. It never starts till after midnight."

We followed the rumble of voices and clattering plates. Deep inside the enormous cellar, people faced a bare wooden stage with two straight-backed chairs, a microphone, and an enormous stylized painting of the white pueblo of Arcos de la Frontera. Above it was a family shrine of sorts—a giant color portrait of Mari Camarena transformed into a radiant flamenco princess with ruby lips and a swirl of taffeta ruffles. Tables were cluttered with tall *tubos* of beer and a bounty of tapas dishes that kept coming, meatballs in tomato sauce, plates piled with french fries.

Mari Camarena was shorter than most people in the room, but she was nevertheless a commanding presence. She bustled rather than walked, high heels clicking on the floor. She was a woman who touched everything, tasted all, plunging ahead. She hovered in the background in the club kitchen, behind a long counter, issuing commands in a husky voice with the strength of crushing rocks. Her relatives—helping out for the night—frantically poured more beer and moved tapas from kitchen to table, banging dishes as clamorously as possible.

Yet she always insisted that she was shy and loathed center stage. At her own club, she habitually enlists others to introduce visiting flamenco singers. On this night, the master of ceremonies was Manuel Zapata, who read his own poetry

before ceding the wooden stage to three visiting female flamenco singers. When the first one began, the guitar player
closed his eyes, losing himself in words of love and betrayal.
A burst of music filled the room and they sang about death
and moonlight and heartbreak.

As the performance continued, the club's general, Mari
Camarena, leaned against a back wall, her face finally relax-
ing with the notes flowing like the river.

I don't know why she was so uneasy with people. Perhaps
that's why she was attracted to *saeta* music. A reluctant performer can melt into a crowd, shunning a stage for the street.
Once I saw a grainy video of her August 1984 singing debut
during the festival of Vela de las Nieves in Arcos de la Frontera. She was young and slender and wore a pure white sleeveless dress, a green flower pinned to her shoulder, and a gold
charm bracelet dangling from one of her tanned arms.

Before she came onstage, the host introduced Mari with
an unusual public plea for the novice performer. "She is very
nervous and anxious," he said, beckoning her to the microphone, where she took refuge in a stiff chair.

But any fears of performing in public didn't exist when
she made her unusual singing choices. Only Mari Camarena
would have the confidence to pick a *petenera* to sing for her
debut. *Petenera* is a form of Spanish blues, a mix of wailing
guitar and weeping voice, a song of sadness and triumph, love
and death.

Some flamencologists date the *petenera* as far back as the

twelfth century in Arcos de la Frontera, and claim that descendants of exiled Jews still sing the *petenera* in the Balkans with a classic verse about *"la perdición de los hombres"* or "the damnation of men." Many Gypsy performers scorn the *petenera* as bad luck, like an actor cursed by playing Macbeth. They refuse to sing or listen to its bitter lyrics, which are barbed with references to a beautiful Jewess, Rebecca, or a missionary of God, likely an inquisitor.

What drew Mari Camarena to the music of suffering like *peteneras* and *saetas*? She was at a loss to explain it. Nor did she spend a lot of time dissecting her musical inspirations. And perhaps that was the point. Maybe I was wrong to look for logic. Music is knowledge that comes from the heart. It comes closest to expressing the inexpressible. When a singer begins a *saeta*, time slows down and the singer enters a world dominated by force, human tragedy, and, above all, individuality. The simple experience of the soul is more important than abstract religious beliefs. Once the music is inside, it never leaves.

"It's something you are born with," she told me. "I have it. My brother doesn't. My children don't sing. To sing a *saeta*, you have to feel emotions stirring inside. If you don't feel anything, then nothing rises from you. If you feel nothing, nothing comes. Now when I try to sing it's almost impossible to stop crying."

Her repertoire ranges from *saetas* and *peterneras* to fandangos, Andalusian folk songs with roots that date back to the Arab invasion in 711, to *serranas*, nineteenth-century parables that romanticize the mountain life of bandits and smugglers in the Sierra de Cádiz.

Mari's preferred stage is the street. But she is extremely particular about finding the right atmosphere. A narrow passageway. Orange blossoms. The huge wooden door of the church of San Pedro. The crystal tears of Nuestra Señora de los Dolores.

"You have to be inspired by the moment," she said. "There are a lot of things that you need for the music to rise from your heart."

She also has her own peculiar preferences for picking the indefinable precise moment to sing during Semana Santa. In the past, her husband, Pedro, was her trusted scout. He pushed a path for her with a heavy camera slung around his neck and her water bottle in his hand. They hunted for places where the air shimmers with candles and people believe in miracles, walking barefoot on cobblestones. They search for moonlight, night stars, and pure white arches. The moment.

Calle de la Corredera? *Nada.* The main thoroughfare that splits Arcos is too wide for a singing voice to carry long distances. Picturesque wrought-iron balconies, so common to Arcos, are also perilous for performances because of the strain of singing powerfully enough to reach people in the streets.

"I feel much safer below in the street," Mari said. "I feel insecure in the balcony because the wind carries away your voice. It also feels so much more lonely there."

It was Pedro's job to roam the crowd, to gauge reaction to Mari's singing. "Sometimes I've heard her *saetas* quiet a crying child," he laughed, "but then the father of the child starts crying."

Yet despite all these idiosyncratic strategies, Mari couldn't save her own voice. A few years ago she started feeling her voice getting hoarse. The high extended notes she attempted when she sang were ragged and scratchy.

"I couldn't hit the notes that I wanted. Other people applauded me, but I knew I wasn't singing my best," she said. "It wasn't my voice, a clean voice, a powerful voice. I couldn't achieve what I wanted."

She sought treatment from a doctor who diagnosed a chronic condition of inflamed vocal cords and recommended an extreme solution.

"I spent all my life singing, and what was the treatment? Speak quietly. Stop singing," she said ruefully.

Saetas were the backdrop of her life. She grew up listening to the Camarenas—her father, Manuel, and uncle, Antonio—singing Semana Santa *saetas* in such similar voices that people swore they heard the same man. She was born in a time that she could absorb it, love it, fear it, and know its secrets. From the moment she sang for her first procession, on a dare at age twelve, it was her sound track.

So the doctor's shock treatment was the equivalent of killing a *golondrina*, the tiny creature whose swelling birdsong is the morning music of Arcos. With maturity, the power of a *saeta* singer's voice deepens and mellows with age and experience. Now in her fifties, Mari has shared only her silence for the last four years during Semana Santa.

"Will you ever sing *saetas* again?" I asked.

"By next Palm Sunday, Easter, I will know."

"How will you know if you are ready after all this time?"

"It's the moment that will tell me."

"Of course."

I think back on her words and wonder if I was drawn to Mari Camarena because I thought she could teach me something about submitting to that earthly force that everyone feels and no sage can explain.

Later I told other people in the pueblo that I intended to follow Mari during Semana Santa, which was still many months away. Perhaps she would never sing again. Some suggested diplomatically that there were better, more talented *saeta* singers to follow. They offered names of other performers. She was just a baker, after all. I listened politely and then flatly rejected the advice.

"No," I said. "I want to be with her. She has not performed for four years. What can be more beautiful than the moment when she breaks her silence?"

SIXTEEN

Return to the Ottoman Empire

Belgrade, 2010

My job as a reporter takes me to unexpected places. Romania and Poland, Serbia and Bosnia and Kosovo, cities in the Balkans like Sarajevo, Pristina, Belgrade—places utterly disconnected from my life. For many people they are places on maps, news headlines about ethnic strife and mass graves, and fugitive war criminals.

But when I arrived in Belgrade in autumn—in search of one of Europe's most wanted war criminal suspects, Ratko Mladić—I was surprised to find a vibrant old quarter with sunny terraces and diners singing with roving Gypsy bands. It felt as if some mystical force were directing me here. The story of the fugitive was complex and absorbing and was nearing the finish when I realized this place had a special resonance for me. There were too many coincidences—the latest two discoveries on my long-running quest to track my ancestors through DNA sampling.

For months, I was unable to identify a single match for my father's Y chromosome signature, haplogroup G, which was one of three types that predominated among Sephardic Jews, according to Spanish and British researchers. On the advice of Bennett Greenspan, president of the Texas-based Family Tree DNA, which I used for testing, I submitted my father's sample for further analysis.

Each analysis cost more money, with periodic promotions offered with breathless discounts. "For a limited time we will offer this test to you at the discounted price of $189, and we will limit the number of orders to 250 on a first come, first served basis."

I signed up to examine more elements on my father's Y chromosome signature and to determine the mitochondrial DNA passed from my grandmother, Angela Chacón, to my father. Sometimes mutations arise in these DNA sequences that provide markers.

Genes are like little islands of information in the DNA sequence. The vast areas between the sequences are known as junk DNA because they have no known function for the organism. But within the junk DNA territory are the markers and mutations that determine relationships. Junk to treasure.

Usually the test results took weeks to arrive. And when

they did come, I needed time to understand exactly what the new information meant. So it took me a while to fathom the news from the DNA testing service that revised the ancestry of my father's male line. On the basis of the new, more detailed information, my father's DNA unexpectedly shifted from haplogroup G to type I, a puzzling change for me.

Typically, haplogroup I is widespread throughout southeastern and central Europe and most common in the west Balkans in Bosnia and Herzegovina and parts of Croatia, with the highest percentage on Hvar, a Croatian island in the Adriatic that stood in the middle of ancient sea routes. Haplogroup members like my father carry a twenty-thousand-year-old marker dubbed M170.

"The change from one nucleotide or 'letter' is rare," Francesc Calafell, the geneticist with the Pompeu Fabra University in Barcelona, explained to me. "Most mutations such as M170 are thought to have happened only once in human history." The testing service had earlier tried to predict my father's haplogroup using a simple formula, but G and I are so close that the preliminary evaluation couldn't detect the difference. By testing actual mutations, they came up with his real haplogroup.

Some of the highest frequencies of haplogroup I are found among Andalusians in the south of Spain, according to data collected by Family Tree DNA and the Sorenson Molecular Genealogy Foundation. Even higher percentages are found in Portuguese border towns where practicing Sephardic Jews were initially welcomed after their exile from Spain in 1492.

In Bragança, thirteen miles from the Spanish border in northern Portugal, sample data showed almost eighteen percent of the male population fell into this I haplogroup, followed by another Spanish border town, Braga, with about twelve percent.

Today there is only a small enclave of practicing Jews in Braga, and they are mostly foreigners. But the legacy of Jewish conversos lives on among its descendants. On the Saturday before Easter, shepherds lead herds of sheep into the center of Castelo de Vide for a blessing. They pray for forgiveness for mistakes they have committed, a legacy of the tradition of the Jewish Day of Atonement, Yom Kippur.

A few weeks after receiving new information about my father's DNA signature, I received more puzzling information from the testing service. They had analyzed my Costa Rican grandmother's DNA signature and the results showed a rare female haplogroup, W. It was information that I filed away and forgot because I was too busy tracking distant generations of male Carvajals.

But as I traveled on assignment, I carried a small laptop computer with all my data about the family, which I would ponder periodically, shifting information like jigsaw pieces searching for the right spot in the puzzle. Shortly before I traveled to Belgrade for a story, I started looking at my grandmother's file and I came again across the information about her haplogroup W.

I learned, to my surprise, that it is a relatively rare European type present in the eastern Baltic region of Estonia,

Latvia, and Lithuania, and in the Ural Mountains of Russia, as well as in Spain, Poland, and Iran. When I compared my grandmother's information with that of other people in the DNA database, I discovered the highest percentage of near matches were with people living in Croatia.

The Balkans? Croatia? Till then I didn't even know the name of the Ural Mountains.

When I squinted toward the distant horizon of women on my grandmother's side, I didn't see any connection. She was born in Costa Rica. Her mother, Anaïs Moya, was born in Cuba in 1885 to a Havana doctor and housewife who later moved to Colombia and ultimately to Costa Rica. Her maternal grandmother, Angela Xiquez, was also Cuban-born, the daughter of Melchor Xiquez, a Spaniard, and his wife, Carmen Jimenez.

When I looked at the male line of my grandmother's father—Julio Chacón—I could see back eleven generations, including a Spaniard who became the mayor of San José, Costa Rica, in 1827. The family tree also included Don Bernardo Sarmiento de Sotomayor y Ponce de León, a Peruvian colonist who became a government registrar in Costa Rica in the eighteenth century.

So what was this odd DNA connection to the Balkans? The likely answer emerged when I stopped in Belgrade at the Jewish Historical Museum, a dark stone building with creaky steps that led to window cases displaying antique Torahs and black-and-white photos of Sephardic Jewish women in ornate embroidered dresses and pillbox hats. A yellowing map, dated from 1492 to 1554, showed the migration path of Sephardic Jews north along the Portuguese and French coasts and then south overland toward Italy to Belgrade and coastal towns of Croatia. Did my grandmother's relatives, who left Spain and scattered through Central and South America, also migrate to the Balkans? It was certainly possible, given that there seemed no other explanation for a DNA test linking my family to people in Croatia.

After the Sephardim were exiled from Spain in 1492, they scattered in five currents. Some crossed the Mediterranean and settled in Morocco. Others took the road to Italy, joining older communities in Rome, Naples, Venice, and Sicily. One wave headed for Portugal, and another to Spanish colonies in the Americas. The largest exodus traveled to Turkey, where they were welcomed by Muslims. They guarded their culture and a fifteenth-century way of speaking Spanish, which was called Ladino. The Romance language, now in danger of extinction, mixed with words from where the exiles traveled and settled: Hebrew, Arabic, Portuguese, French, Turkish, Greek, Bulgarian, Bosnian, and Serbo-Croatian.

During the fifteenth and sixteenth centuries, the Ottoman Empire reached the zenith of its power, and its sultans Bayezid II, Mehmet II, and Suleiman the Magnificent offered refuge to Jewish outcasts as an investment in their own economy. They valued the skills of Jewish artisans, craftsmen, and merchants who had knowledge and connections, and who became pioneers of global commerce.

When the Spanish sovereigns Ferdinand and Isabella expelled the Jews, Bayezid II mocked them: "You call Ferdinand a wise king? He who impoverishes his country and enriches our own?" As other countries turned on Jews, Ottoman leaders relied on them to open trade routes. Tragedy fostered opportunity. The Lisbon massacres in 1506 provoked the migration of thousands of Portuguese conversos east to what is now Turkey. Ultimately, they helped establish Jewish communities along all of the important trade routes from the West to Turkey. Some of the enclaves, I discovered, were Jews' Street in Dubrovnik, Croatia, and the Jewish quarter in Sarajevo.

When I glimpsed Sarajevo for the first time on the same reporting trip, it was still pocked with bullet holes from the Balkan war of 1992–1995, when fugitive ex-general Ratko Mladić orchestrated a siege from the surrounding hills, with sniper bullets and mortar shells. More than ten thousand people died during that period, thirty-five hundred of them children.

The melancholy mood of estrangement is still palpable here among people who refuse to forget. Is this a better way of dealing with history than amnesia? I wondered. Within the old city, footsteps from my hotel was the flickering eternal flame for a World War II memorial and then red splashes of "Sarajevo roses" embedded deep in the cobblestones.

These scars—crevices filled with red resin—are symbols of the killing spots where mortar shells landed. The Markale market, now teeming with stands of vegetable and fish sellers, is marked with red resin petals from the explosion of a single 122-millimeter mortar shell that in 1994 killed sixty-eight people. In the wooden stalls in Sarajevo's old quarter of Baščaršija, I noticed baskets of recycled artillery and mortar shell casings transformed into what they call "trench art"— bullet pens, key chains, and necklaces.

At one point, Sarajevo was a crossroads in the Balkans for Jewish communities and was nicknamed Little Jerusalem. Along the western slopes of Mount Trebević, outside Sarajevo, is a Sephardic Jewish burial ground founded in 1630. During the siege of Sarajevo, the rows of Sephardic tombstones were the front line for much of the fighting, one of the main artillery positions for the Bosnian Serb snipers attacking Bosnian Muslims, who dominate Sarajevo.

The Ohel, a cemetery structure whose name means "tent," was shelled and burned in 1994, and ninety-five percent of the graves were damaged. When the Bosnian Serbs withdrew, they also planted land mines, which were later cleared with funding from the United States government.

In Sarajevo's historic quarter, artisans sell hand-hammered copper art that carry the obscure symbols of Sarajevo. At one store, I browsed the shelves of artworks with Dan Bilefsky, a fellow journalist who worked with me on the war criminal story.

We looked at delicate pictures of ringed door knockers and a hammered portrait of a house-shaped gravestone engraved with a series of symbols, horses, and human figures. Dan bought them both from the artist, who explained that the door knocker is a symbol of Sarajevo. Then Dan handed me the door knocker as a surprise gift for our shared adventure of searching for Ratko Mladić.

It was only as we were driving away toward Srebrenica— the burial site for more than eight thousand Muslim men and boys massacred by Serb forces in 1995—that we realized we had not asked the artist the meaning of the symbols that would later hang in our homes.

I couldn't decode it, much as I couldn't understand the puzzle of my own family's branches and DNA clues that led to the Balkans. The reality, though, is that most religious authorities and government institutions consider clues in the blood meaningless. As Dr. Calafell, the Spanish geneticist, told me, ancestry is made up of many individuals and the results tell only one version.

Rabbi Nissan Ben Avraham, whom I met in the Jewish quarter of Barcelona and advises converso descendants, also is not impressed with DNA sample testing.

"I don't know if DNA proves much," he said, noting that genetic evidence of ancestry is a much smaller part of the politically charged debate in Israel about how to define and authorize legitimate Jewish conversions. "The problem is that DNA is not sufficient to demonstrate the mother of the mother of the mother and so on. I take it more seriously when someone says, 'I want to know about Judaism.' That's not a problem for me. But when you look for evidence, it has to be very weighty."

In the last few years, the Spanish government has granted a special right of return to Sephardic Jews who can prove their ancestors were expelled from Iberia. Ordinarily it takes ten years of residency in Spain for a foreigner to qualify for citizenship, but the government has reduced the time to two years for descendants of Sephardic Jews. In Turkey, which was a refuge for thousands of Jews in the fifteenth century as part of the Ottoman Empire, descendants have been using a new amendment to Spain's civil code to obtain citizenship in Europe without moving there. Turkish lawyers have helped people apply for citizenship through a category of special cases that does not require the two-year residency. The appeal is a Spanish passport—essentially entry to the European Union—which allows Turkish residents to move freely through Europe without the bureaucratic hassles of obtaining visas for travel on Turkish passports.

To prove their ancestry, descendants must obtain a document of origin from Turkey's chief rabbinate and then submit their application to the Spanish Justice Ministry. For the ministry, some clues are found in surnames, which often represent a place, a flower, a fruit tree, or some aspect of nature.

I had so focused on science and DNA that I had overlooked everyday symbols as basic as a last name. When I spread out our family tree in front of me, I saw names of ancestors that hinted at long-forgotten stories. My grandmother's name, Chacón, means "salamander," a symbol that baffled me until I read that the slender amphibian is described in the Talmud as a powerful creature generated in fire and capable of protecting others from flames.

As I scanned the list, the last names formed a vivid tapestry of places and plants. My cousin's last name, Valverde, is from the name of a town in Portugal meaning "green valley." On my grandmother's ancestral line, there were Alcázar, "fortress"; Sarmiento, "vine shoot"; Policar, "thumb"; and Umana, "who is like God."

Most of the various spellings of Carvajal—Carbajal, Carballo, Carabello, Caravallo—mean "oak tree" or "forest of oaks." But one variation, Carajal, describes my general mood.

Rejected. A place not in order.

SEVENTEEN

A Time to Speak

Arcos de la Frontera, 2009

For weeks, I tried to pin down Mari on whether she would sing again for Semana Santa.

Back home in France, I called her house and listened to her ambivalent answers, detecting a hint of scratchiness in her staccato Spanish. Though I was disappointed, I understood her doubts. But still I made plans to join Mari and her husband, Pedro, for Holy Week just in case they suddenly decided it was the moment for her street comeback.

When my family and I returned to Arcos and our ex-bordello—slightly green in the courtyard from fungus that attacked white walls during winter rainstorms—I tracked her down.

"Call me on Domingo de Ramos—Palm Sunday," she said, fending me away yet again. And so I started to accept that this would not be the year for the singing revival of Mari's fragile voice.

On the morning of Palm Sunday, I called her again, but no one answered. I gave up, vaguely embarrassed, because I was beginning to feel like a stalker. Perhaps my calls were making her uneasy, pushing her to use a delicate voice in need of mending. So I told my husband I did not expect to see her. We left that morning on our own to trail the first of ten brotherhoods that would march throughout the week.

My neighbor, María José, and two of her three sons, Pablo and Juan, were members of the first marching brotherhood, La Borriquita, the youngest *cofradía*, dating back to 1962. I think it's the most buoyant and joyous group because they march from the little church of María Auxiliadora with faces uncovered, veils thrown back. The women, dressed in white robes, wave palms woven with red ribbons. Along with them are young boys dressed as Roman soldiers with golden helmets topped by curling red plumes. The *costaleros* struggle under the weight of a *paso* that bears an image of Christ riding a plaster donkey, *la borriquita*, and clutching a red rose.

We arrived in time to see a veiled María José commanding her legion of boy soldiers, who sliced the air with plastic swords and shields and fell into step on her orders. Along the sidewalks, some mothers pushed babies in strollers, also dressed in red veils and white robes.

María José's oldest son, Sergio, had started marching at

five years of age and continued until he was twelve. She was
enlisted as commander of the Romanitos when the previous
leader retired and there wasn't a willing replacement. She
was thrilled to see the boys marching as the image of Christ
was carried slowly out of the church every year.

"I'm proud of my work and, most important, I'm proud of
the boys. It would have been really sad to lose the tradition,"
she told me. Yet she said she does not consider herself a regular churchgoer: "I believe that faith is what everyone has. I
believe in God, but I don't go much to church. I believe faith
is something inside and that it's not necessary to attend mass
to have faith."

When we first moved across the street from María José,
I didn't know what to make of her. I was so accustomed to
living in a neighborhood in France where stone walls inhib-
ited friendships. I didn't even know the name of the French
woman who lived next door to us for seven years. So I nicknamed my frosty neighbor Madame Sunshine. And when she
moved away, with the moving van parked in front of our
driveway without permission, Madame Sunshine left without
a word of good-bye.

In contrast, in southern Andalusia, María José introduced
herself as soon as we moved in. I soon realized through the
sheer force of her dynamic personality that she was battling
the Spanish economic crisis. She was in her thirties, tiny and
opinionated, with thick reddish-brown hair and dark eyes
that sparkled or sparked, depending on whether you crossed
her. Where others in Arcos talked about art and spirituality,

she talked about reality. She had married much too young and moved into her first house when there still was no electricity. Of all the people I met in Arcos, she was the purest Andalusian. Friendly. Blunt. Warm. Profane. Cynical. Needy. Generous. She practically adopted my daughter, inviting her for sleepovers, though my daughter's Spanish was imperfect and María José's English nonexistent. Her sons didn't seem to mind having a girl around, and my daughter was thrilled.

"I am her Spanish mother," María José told me many times, and I was grateful.

There was a practical side to María José, who found solace in the church. When her husband lost his job and they needed aid to hold her family of five together, she turned to one of the more humble churches in Arcos on the outskirts of the old quarter. In turn, she volunteered to help clean the church and organize the Palm Sunday Romanitos.

For María José, the hardness of life softened with street processions that ushered in the dawn with promises of redemption. Pain is purification. Suffering in Andalusia is a demonstration of courage and endurance. And María José needed its comfort. As La Crisis deepened, she told me later, one bleak Christmas she had only two euros for five people. Perhaps, in part because of dire need, there has been a marked revival of Holy Week festivities in the south of Spain, where Andalusia is known as the land of Semana Santa.

Life is stark here, so death is shown with all its grim reality. On Good Fridays in Arcos, the Brotherhood of Holy

Burial carries an enormous gilded glass coffin with an image of the body of Christ. The form is rigid, muscles contracted, and face mottled with livid colors. Blood seeps from the wounds. The figure reflects the essential character of Spain: serious, strong, deeply emotional.

The penitents follow the coffin in black, flowing tunics and matching peaked hoods. They are a chilling sight: hundreds of men in black marching down a hill toward Calle de la Corredera with the flickering light of candles. They move in utter silence, brushing against the crowd and delivering commands to move aside. The earliest roots of the processions date back as far as 1420 to a village in the Sierra Morena where people performed acts of penance in the streets in fear of a coming apocalypse. The Black Death had provoked a dementia of despair that also ravaged Arcos.

The memory still endures with a celebration every year on the Día de Voto, or Day of Supplication. It marked the moment in 1649 when, after nine years, the plague vanished from the pueblo. The disappearance was credited to the cloistered nuns from the convent of the Mercedarias Descalzas, who prayed for this miracle until, according to legend, a painting of Christ glowed in their tiny chapel. In the chaos of plague, poverty, and hunger, the only hope for people who suffered short, miserable lives was the drama of Jesus. They shared the same daily injustices and suffering. With a brotherhood, they confronted fear together. And today, when a child is born in Arcos, people say, "Now Christ has a new member of the brotherhood."

Not surprisingly, some brotherhoods became refuges for conversos and secret Jews who sought to mask their religion. Yet every New Year in Arcos, it was the duty of the Brotherhood of the Sweet Name of Jesus to deliver the names of hidden Jews who were suspected of practicing their religion.

This history, though, seems far removed from the daily lives of people who participate in modern rituals. Sinister symbols have no significance anymore. Once I asked Cristóbal, the owner of the Hotel Real de Veas, the meaning of the peaked hoods, or *capirotes*, worn by *nazarenos* parading by his hotel.

"They have always worn them," he replied vaguely.

My Spanish was too weak to argue this point eloquently.

"Are you sure? It must be a symbol of something."

"I don't know. They have always worn them."

I was not satisfied with the answer. There are endless varieties of uses for the *capirotes*, which in Arcos are peaked, stiff cones unlike the squared-off hoods of Seville. One interpretation is that the cones symbolize the reach toward the heavens, like the lime-green cedar trees that are typically planted in Spanish cemeteries. But they were also used by inquisitors and forced on converso Jews accused of practicing their religion in secret. Today the humiliation endures in Spanish expressions: *"Ser un tonto de capirote."* To be an idiot worthy of a dunce cap.

As twilight descended on the old quarter in Arcos de la Frontera, my husband and I pressed into a crowd of people gathering by the church of San Pedro near the Callejón de las Monjas. I checked my telephone again for messages from Mari Camarena or her husband, but it was silent. The crowd around me moved against each other for the best vantage points outside the enormous wooden doors of the church. More people were coming up the hill to wedge their way into the street. I saw María José with her youngest son, Pablo, and she guided us toward the best vantage point with the unerring determination of a frontier scout. She was in a grim mood as we stood there waiting, worrying whether La Crisis would ever break.

"There is no future here for my boys," she said, shaking her head. "Maybe we need to move to another country."

The gloom was catching. But the future was momentarily forgotten when we saw the crowd part and heard a burst of horns tipped to the sky. There is always a sense of danger and thrill at this moment. We were waiting for a seven-foot platform carrying the statue to squeeze through the doors of the church, and then be carried down dozens of narrow steps. Thirty to sixty *costaleros* are crouched underneath the *paso*, a canopy covering them. They strained under the weight of a *paso* with a humbled figure of Christ with his hands tied and behind him a Roman soldier and Judas, with a little bag of silver clutched in his hand.

The *costaleros* rely on a distinct hierarchy to navigate the hazards, sweeping past walls within inches. The *capataz*, a member of one of the local political parties with ambitions to be the pueblo's mayor, directs the men with brisk commands. He was dressed in a suit, his face shiny with sweat and tension, constantly checking street angles. He made one sharp knock against the *paso* for a warning, two to stop, and three to lift the *paso* high.

El Prendimiento—the Capture of Christ—is the name of this brotherhood, a relatively young one dating to 1946. The procession moved so slowly that there was time to pass ahead and wait at one of the tapas bars, Mesón El Patio, for the *paso* to arrive. My husband and I weaved through a crowd with the same idea to place an order for a drink.

There I spotted Mari Camarena at a table, smiling serenely with her husband, Pedro. She was dressed in a cream-colored jacket with matching pearl earrings and carrying a hand-tooled leather purse. Pedro was toting a bottle protectively, as if it were brimming with holy water.

I made my way to their side through people crowded at the bar, below dangling sides of ham. Kisses all around. This was a tense moment for Mari after waiting for four years to break her silence, and I could read the anxiety on her face. Pedro also seemed apprehensive.

For me, Mari represented a grand legacy of ancient, subversive voices, though I am sure she would hardly agree with me. For her, the past had no bearing. My family showed the same attitude after they fled Spain for the New World, settling in Costa Rica, where they mastered the art of living with dual identities.

Saeta music was a coded form of singing with double meanings, the music of converso Jews conveying their true emotions in words demonstrating faith in Christianity. Those codes are long forgotten by contemporary *saeta* performers, who sing from the soul without fully knowing why.

I wondered if those ancient voices could reach me through Mari's notes. I wanted the music to plunge me into the past, which is equally as real as the present on the cobblestones of Arcos de la Frontera. Could I share the pain and memory of desperate conversos?

Physics teaches us something remarkable about connecting to the past. Every action in the past and future is implicit in the current moment. All events—past, present, and future—exist statically in a four-dimensional universe of time. So if my ancestors are dead, this period of time is no greater a reality than when they lived. Albert Einstein, the German-born theoretical physicist who developed the theory of general relativity, took comfort from this concept of time when a lifelong friend died. "Now he has departed from this strange world a little ahead of me," Einstein said. "That means nothing. People like us, who believe in physics, know that the distinction between past, present, and future is only a stubbornly persistent illusion."

Could I reach back through the vast spaces of memory? Outside, the moon made shadows of orange trees along the narrow alley. The night was heavy with the fragrance of blossoms, spiced with incense and burning wax.

"Are you ready?" I asked Mari.

"It has to feel right."

"But where?"

"I will know."

As we spoke, the owner of Mesón El Patio interrupted Mari and Pedro and shouted above the din of the crowd in his bar: "They're coming."

I bolted, following Mari and Pedro. They pushed their way to the street outside. She forged ahead, carrying her purse primly hooked on her arm, and we could hear the slow beat of the drums and the trumpets of the musical group, Christ of the Good Death. Mari checked the wind, shaking her head. She stood briefly in one spot and then paced along a narrow passageway to take refuge by a wall.

"Are you nervous?" Pedro asked.

"No. . . . Maybe."

"You are really brave," Pedro said to comfort her.

The drums grew louder, and in the distance we could see the swaying image of Christ with bound hands, the statue of Our Father, Jesus of the Sovereign Power. The red *paso* was led by masked men in red hoods and white robes from the brotherhood of the Tres Caídas—Three Falls—with huge brass incense holders carried aloft on poles. The penitents carried tall white tapers in their hands, the wax dripping on the cobblestone. There was just enough flame to see the glitter of eyes within hooded masks.

"Now I am nervous."

I studied her, watching her dig deep. I could see a memory flicker across her face as she disappeared somewhere into the past. Pedro offered her the water bottle to wet her throat, but she rejected it, too distracted.

She had told me before that as a singer grows old, abilities fade. But experience enhances the music. "A singer has to suffer," she told me. The *saeta*," she said, "is a song of pain."

I knew instinctively she was thinking about her father and uncle. "I always listened to them singing *saetas* and flamenco," she said. "When you are very young, the feelings are not the same. But as I grew older, when I would sing I would weep. Sometimes my tears wouldn't stop. I was too caught up in the passions of the street, the images, the people."

The drumbeat was growing louder and I felt a shiver as I watched the men in peaked hoods and robes approaching. I could only imagine what Mari was thinking. The *paso* with its image of a bound Jesus was rocking toward us.

She had chosen a spot earlier to sing on a rise above Alcaraván, Don Manuel's old haunt, named for the city's clan of poets from the 1950s. I watched Mari taking sips from her water bottle and mentally warming up. On a curt command of the *capataz*, the *costaleros* gingerly lowered the *paso* just in front of her. But before she started, another man stepped forward. She receded back in the crowd, watching him sing to the image, his work-worn hands outstretched and his voice rising.

"Who is that?" Mari's husband asked no one in particular. "He's not a *saetero*."

One of their friends walked by and whispered the same critique: "That is not a *saetero.*"

I was not sure what exactly they meant, other than that his voice seemed to veer into a forced cry.

When he finished, Pedro nodded at the *capataz*. I glanced at Mari, whose eyes were closed, almost in meditation. Then it happened—she raised her hands, and her voice sliced through the night with a sharp arrow of pain: *Ahi ahii aheeeeeee.*

"My Christ, / My Christ, / Flee this capture. / Your courage is so sad. / Not your hands."

Her voice was not perfect, straining on the high notes. But now I heard the difference from the other singer. Her words were wrenched hard from the soul. I could hear distant echoes of the voices of others, of pain and longing, flowing like the Guadalete from past to present. Tears came to my eyes. I brushed them away, surprised at my own emotions.

When Mari's last notes faded away in the darkness, applause erupted from the sidewalk. Some shouted, *"¡Da le! ¡Da le!"*—the Spanish equivalent of "All right!"

A man rushed toward her, pressing a crumpled slip of paper into her hands. It contained verses of a *saeta* titled "Our Lady of Pain."

"You carry a dagger in your breast, / My Lady of Pain. / Your arms were made / For the best of the best."

Mari slipped the note in her purse. There was no time to savor the applause, although the daughter and grandson of the late *cronista*, Don Manuel, were nearby and pressed her with kisses.

"It's always magic for me." She smiled.

"*Vámonos.* Let's go." Pedro urged her onward.

She gripped her purse and I followed the two of them, with no idea where we were headed. We pushed through the crowd, who reached out to touch the *paso.* To my shock, Pedro made his way through the crowd toward the Chapel of Mercy, the ancient synagogue, banished from the pueblo's memory.

The mayor of Arcos de la Frontera and Manuel, son of the *saeta* singer Zapata, were waiting in the street. Inside, the bloodied image of Christ on a cross was laid down in the center of a table with the image of Our Lady of the Seven Sorrows facing the figure. His form was crosshatched with delicate cuts. Sometimes I wondered why this pueblo of secrets is so preoccupied with blood. They put it in their curses, and eat it in *morcilla,* a thick sausage stuffed with rice.

I stared up at the vaulted ceilings of the Chapel of Mercy with hexagrams that date back to the Seal of Solomon and the city of Jerusalem. I gazed at the intricate stone carving of a snake coiling toward a Jew—or is it a slave? Mari has told me numerous times that she knows nothing about the Jewish roots of *saeta* music. Her music is pure emotion, basic instinct.

"I sing like I know how to sing. I repeat: A *saeta* is a *saeta* is a *saeta,* and a prayer and nothing more."

But why were we here? I looked across the crucifix to Mari, who was raising her hands to sing again, eyes closed in rapture. Men and women surrounded her, silent, as if in a hypnotic state, except for a young boy who was jerked back by his father as he tried to finger the rich black-and-gold dress of Our Lady of the Seven Sorrows.

A burst of aching music shook the room and Mari wrapped her voice around the pain, drawing out the syllables. Her husband was about to weep amid whispers rising that soothed like a cool mountain stream. A woman at her side was beating her breast. I strained to understand the words, which eluded me except for one clear line. It jolted me as I gazed at the green stars of the old synagogue.

"Take my shoulder," she sang, her hands raised high. "Take my shoulder to bear the burden."

Then I thought of what Manuel Zapata told me earlier that night as we watched the brotherhood marching by with images. "Everything has a meaning, the stars in the crown, the tears in the eyes, the seven daggers piercing the heart of the Virgin. Everything."

I make my living in facts, but it was only then, in the middle of a synagogue in a small town in southern Spain where I was searching for the roots of my family, that I was convinced that we were being directed by spirits chained to the streets and asking for a little relief from the burden.

EIGHTEEN

Decoding Defiance

Arcos de la Frontera, 2010

Cryptic messages are scattered throughout Arcos de la Frontera. Symbols of dignity and defiance. Yet I walked by them without seeing, too focused on facts and traditional reporting. I conducted interviews, read documents, and analyzed records. And then I drew conclusions. My private little newspaper of the buried past.

But I yearned to dig deeper, and Manuel Zapata unknowingly gave me the clue: all the symbols in Arcos de la Frontera are speaking. Persecution forces secret communication. It provokes a unique form of creativity, truth delivered between the lines to careful observers.

The messages are mingled in dark oil paintings of the

Virgin Mary and extravagant *retablos*, the altarpieces of wood, carved with saints and sinners, that dominate church sanctuaries all over Spain. They linger deep in the tones of La Nona, the fifteenth-century bell that tolls for freedom every hour.

These were the symbols that beleaguered Jews and conversos discreetly used to counter an onslaught of powerful propaganda against them that surfaced in European art and Catholic churches. From the eleventh century onward, the artistic representation of Jews intensified into vile images carved into hard stone.

In Paris, I often passed the portal of the Cathedral of Notre Dame, where two classic female figures stand. They are Ecclesia and Synagoga, medieval symbols of Christianity's triumph over Judaism. Across Europe, the images also appear in stained-glass windows, paintings, and prayer books. Ecclesia represents Christianity, a crowned maiden holding a cross. Synagoga is the symbol of Judaism, blindfolded and holding a broken Old Testament tablet in her hand.

Anti-Jewish imagery is carved in the Basilica of San Vicente in Ávila, Spain. Below the church's main arch are carvings that illustrate the sixth-century martyrs Vicente and his sisters, Sabina and Cristeta, who died defending their Christianity. The first scene shows pagan soldiers torturing them to renounce their faith, crushing their heads in a wooden press with the aid of a bearded Jew. The second scene shows the same Jewish figure ensnared by an enormous serpent, prompting him to beg forgiveness and convert to Christianity.

The worst images spread from Germany in the thirteenth century to churches in France and Switzerland and Sweden. The Judensau, German for "Jew's sow," depicted scenes of Jews suckling a pig or examining body parts. The images were carved on the outer walls of medieval churches like the Regensburg cathedral in Germany. It showed Jews in pointed hats surrounding a pig. The sculpture faced the former Jewish quarter of Neupfarrplatz, where cellars were equipped with secret doors that allowed residents to flee to other houses to escape mob pogroms, usually sparked on Good Friday at Easter.

A few years ago, the Regensburg cathedral placed a plaque that offered a cryptic explanation. "This sculpture needs to be seen in its historical context." Such excuses are common at sensitive historical sites, including Arcos.

After the pueblo restored the old synagogue, Capilla de Misericordia, a sign appeared in the interior. It referred to "inappropriate" use of the fifteenth-century building to store religious *pasos* or platforms. But what was inappropriate? The sign didn't explain. Nor was there any information about the history of the building as a synagogue.

How did Jewish conversos counter medieval propaganda? Spanish poet Luis de Góngora wrote that the true meaning of text and symbols could be read only by those with the ability to cast away a shell and discover hidden meaning.

One subversive form that flourished in sixteenth-century Spain was the picaresque novel, a popular genre that chronicled the adventures of low-class rogues who navigated through corrupt Spanish society. Converso writers used the dregs of Spanish life—thieves, prostitutes, beggars, petty criminals—to deliver messages with dual meanings. The characters were worthless in honorable society so they could get away with cynical observations about lecherous priests and immoral aristocrats.

The books could be read literally or with a "third ear" for satire, insinuations, and inside gossip that exposed a hidden, culture-coded world of Marranos. Christians could read the novel one way, whereas conversos could detect something else, deciphering secret messages.

During the long Inquisition, Marrano culture evolved into the art of twisting overt and covert meanings, leaving it to readers in the know to search for double meanings. This also had a profound effect on converso writers and artists, living life on two levels, shifting between concealed inner thoughts and daily actions.

Great literature, according to some historians, was the result.

The most skilled at this game of double meanings was Miguel de Cervantes, the author of the classic *Don Quixote de la Mancha*, the seventeenth-century novel that is considered the most influential work of literature from the Spanish Golden Age. Numerous books have been published in Spain that explore clues to his life and his novel that indicate that he was descended from a converso Jewish family.

Researchers combed for the same clues that I sought about my ancestors. Family. Occupations. Eating habits. Funeral rituals. In his case, Cervantes was a tax collector and his father a surgeon, traditional trades of Jews during the Middle Ages.

Cervantes never mentions eating pork except once, when he refers to dining on Saturdays on *duelos y quebrantos*, or "sorrow and loss." The double meaning is that on the Sabbath he is eating a dish of scrambled eggs and bacon. Some scholars suspect this is a specific recipe that forced converts to demonstrate loyalty to their new religion.

The classic opening line of Cervantes's novel has also been thoroughly dissected for hidden meanings: "Somewhere in La Mancha, in a place I do not care to remember, a gentleman lived not long ago, one of those who has a lance and ancient shield on a shelf and keeps a skinny nag and a greyhound for racing." Some historians consider this vague reference to a region and to *mancha* ("blemish" or "stain") as a code for the mark or stain of being a convert.

The same coded defiance is also carved into *retablos*. These intricate altars with their lifelike images are a fixture in Spain, scattered among churches, cloisters, cathedrals, and mansions. They are the central message in a church sanctuary, reflecting the national character: rugged, strong, extravagant. The hand-painted wooden sculptures tap the deepest religious feelings in Spain, where there is no separation between daily and divine life.

Christian generals carried *retablos* into war against the Moors during the thirteenth century. Warriors prayed to them for protection before plunging into battle, and priests credited them with miracles. The carved wooden figures of saints and sinners were colored to be as human-looking as possible. *Retablos*, as one artist put it, had the power to "lend wings to the souls of those who wear chains on their feet."

The highest-paid artists for the *retablos*—which could take years to finish—were the *encarnadores*, or body painters, and the *doradores*, who applied the gold leaf. Their financial contracts detailed with precision the qualities and costs of complexions for different images. The dewy skin of a young woman for the Virgin Mary. The tint of an infant's color for Christ. The weathered face of Saint John the Evangelist.

One of the most prized painters was Abraham de Salinas, a fourteenth-century Jewish artist who, with his son, was commissioned by four different churches to paint *retablos*. Two years after the pogroms erupted in 1391 against Jews, he received a steady series of commissions for altarpieces in Zaragoza, where Jews had been spared the violence that shattered Barcelona and Seville. These altarpieces included personal references of his own: Saint John the Evangelist is depicted as a Jewish high priest on Yom Kippur, addressing an angel.

Juan de Levi was another accomplished fourteenth-century artist and converso from Zaragoza, who painted the altarpiece of Santa Catalina, San Lorenzo, and San Prudencio for the Tarazona cathedral and was famed for the delicacy of the faces he painted in rich colors. In the same city, Miguel Jiménez and Martín Bernat created *The Altarpiece of the True Cross*, which shows a subservient Jew, Judas, before Queen

Helena with a double meaning: it also could be read as Inquisition interrogation and torture.

Wealthy patrons who commissioned *retablos* worked closely with artists, spelling out in detail their own visions. In Arcos de la Frontera, many *retablos* were funded by rich nobles who hoped that by paying for these pieces of artwork they could secure a place in heaven. The largest one rises to the vaulted ceiling of the church of Santa María, which closed for two years to restore the opulent sixteenth-century *retablo,* which is topped by a fatherly God with a dark, curly beard drifting down a ripple of robes.

There are *retablos* in most of the churches in Arcos, including a local hotel in the *casco antiguo* that was the mansion of the Marqués de Torresoto and the convent of cloistered nuns, whose altarpiece was created in gratitude for their prayers to end the Black Plague. But in modern times, the hard-pressed pueblo has been unable to maintain them all.

A spat erupted when dueling political parties discovered that rats had burrowed behind the *retablo* of San Agustín, a church that was a sixteenth-century center for scholars of philosophy. It bore the symbol of the Jerusalem cross carried by Christian crusaders a thousand years ago. The local newspaper reported with outrage that rodents had gnawed on carnations laid next to an image of Nuestro Padre Jesús Nazareno, the most venerated image of Christ in the pueblo. But the repair cost was staggering for a city reeling with the economic crisis: 400,000 euros—more than half a million dollars.

It took me some time to find hidden messages in the *retablos*. When I walked by them, I was dazzled by the grand scenes but failed to notice precise details—probably the strategy of the original artists. But when I studied them in photographs, some figures emerged with striking expressions that seemed to be speaking.

Two of the most disturbing *retablos* in Arcos had been funded as a gift to the officers of the Inquisition by a wealthy converso Jew, Diego Núñez de Castilla. He was accused by the Inquisition of secretly practicing Judaism, which could have meant punishment as severe as death or elaborate forms of humiliation of the victim and generations of descendants.

With the lowest level of punishment, lapsed conversos were forced to wear a coned hat and sack robes in yellow and orange—the colors of criminals and undesirables. They were called *sambenitos* and paraded barefoot and bare-legged through the streets. Then the robes were draped on the interior walls of the church of Santa María in Arcos. For years, they were marked with the family names of the conversos, a grim warning to descendants who might have harbored hopes of continuing to practice religious rituals in secret.

To reconcile with the Inquisition, Diego Núñez de Castilla donated two *retablos* of undressed souls fighting and clawing their way out of a fiery purgatory. They writhe in the flames of purification to reach a radiant Jesus and God in the heavens. One altar screen is crowded with primitive figures that reach toward San Miguel, the archangel and patron saint of Arcos. At the top of a cornice is a figure of a man kneeling next to San Francisco. It is clearly Núñez de Castilla, bowing to the zealous founder of the Franciscan order that presided over the Inquisition in Spain along with the Dominicans, the black-clad friars whose Latin nickname—*"Domini canes"*—was a pun that summed up their reputation: the hounds of God.

The second *retablo* is more refined. Lifelike, ruddy figures with finely carved muscles beseech a swooping angel for rescue. Above them hovers San Miguel holding the green cross of the Inquisition, the symbol of his mission to empty purgatory and form an invincible army of souls for the Roman Catholic Church.

The panicky expressions of the figures drew me closer. One exceptional figure seemed immune to the frenzy. At the front, in a corner, is an image of a bearded man with a quizzical expression that made me question myself.

Beards are often a code for Jews, because during the early fifteenth century a series of repressive laws in Spain were introduced in the name of the child king John II. Jews were forced to live in enclosed ghettos and barred from trimming hair or beards, to better identify them among other Spaniards. Typically bearded figures were placed in the front of *retablos*, near the center, and were often used as a symbol of evil. In both of these altarpieces, the bearded figure is placed in exactly the same spot: on the right, gazing forward with a similar expression of detachment from other wretched souls.

I couldn't look away. As I stared at the figure, one question overwhelmed me: What are you saying, Diego Núñez?

The dark flesh tint of the bearded figure is subdued. There are touches of carmine—a red color boiled from insects—on the lips, nostrils, eyebrows, and hair. There is a general effect of power and dignity amid the misery of purgatory. "I endure this," it seemed to say, "but I do not belong."

What did the clues mean? Did the location of the image on the right signal righteousness?

Think, I reminded myself. Don't ask.

The altarpiece is installed in the Church of San Francisco, which played a central role in the Inquisition. It was home to the Franciscan brothers. The Brotherhood of the Sweet Name of Jesus, one of the oldest *cofradías* in Arcos, was tied to the church and worked closely with the Franciscans, carrying the church's images in processions during Semana Santa. On January 2 of every year, it was the task of a special elite dozen members of the brotherhood, Los Doce de la Hermandad, to denounce neighbors who blasphemed the name of Jesus.

The Franciscans staged Inquisition tribunals a short walk away. The table for trials was set up in a plaza, presided over by two *comisarios* and local bailiffs from the wealthy family of the Marqués de Torresoto. Members of Los Doce de la Hermandad were at their side.

Along a side street, facing the plaza, stands a white house that still carries the name it had at that time: the Casa de Angustias, the House of Anguish. It was the home in 1692 of Pedro Acosta, the converso hat maker and linen merchant whose father, Isahak de Acosta, a prominent rabbi, had written the book *Divine Conjectures*. The younger Acosta, a wealthy property owner in Arcos, was ruined by inquisitors after witnesses reported him for heresy. His friends betrayed him, confessing under pressure that together father and son had followed the "Law of Moses." Acosta, sixty-two, had aroused suspicions by failing to doff his hat while passing a religious image of Christ near the chapel of San Juan de Dios, according to Inquisition records of his trial in Seville. A priest also claimed that Acosta blessed himself suspiciously with holy water, tossing water over his shoulders to avoid tapping himself.

Why did Diego Núñez commission two altarpieces devoted to purgatory to pay off his debts to inquisitors? One explanation is that wealthy Spanish nobles paid indulgences to the Church to skip purgatory, to buy a shortcut into heaven. Or perhaps it is a concept that Jews believed—according to the Old Testament—that good acts could rescue the souls of the deceased.

As I studied the frantic souls in the Diego Núñez *retablo*, I noticed that most of the denizens of purgatory were nude, with ruddy-colored skin that matched the flames licking around them. Then I noticed something that made me laugh out loud in the silent church. No one was nearby, so it didn't matter. In the dimness of the sanctuary and across the centuries, Diego Nuñez was sharing a private joke that was in plain sight.

How could I have missed Diego Núñez's last laugh? The punch line: hats and haircuts.

Flailing in the flames is a man with a bishop's miter. Then I noticed another figure with the tonsured haircut of a monk. A third wears the stiff hat of a cardinal. The most desperate figure is a half-naked man crowned with a distinctive papal tiara, the three-tiered *triregnum*. On the left in this writhing mass is a woman with a golden crown—a reference, perhaps, to Queen Isabella, who expelled the Jews and forced them to convert?

For all eternity, Diego Núñez had told these religious luminaries to go to hell. Art historian Marc Michael Epstein, a religious studies professor at Vassar College, believes that Jewish artists countered grim tableaus attacking Jews with symbols in art and illuminated manuscripts that had different connotations for Christians and Jews.

Dragons or great primordial serpents were a symbol of intellect for Jewish artists, a way of telegraphing an image of justice. The rabbit—which was a medieval anti-Semitic reference to Jews who "multiplied like rabbits"—was transformed into a benevolent symbol that resonated with Jews and conversos: a swift, canny animal that could escape the hunters.

In the same Church of San Francisco, across from Núñez's altarpiece, is a moody work that is my favorite painting in Arcos. Called *The Allegory of the Inquisition*, it was painted by an unknown artist or artists. Over the centuries it has taken on a life of its own, retouched to mask odious symbols that fell out of favor.

The Virgin Mary is ascending in a drift of blue robes through golden clouds bordered by cherubs. To her right are a king and a queen brandishing swords and underscored in gold with the line "We with our weapons." To the Virgin's left are the princes of the Church, with feather quills in their hands and the words "We with our pens." San Francisco kneels below the Virgin with a gift that has been retouched by someone who seethed with resentment. The green cross of the Inquisition that he held in his hands has been masked with a golden brooch. A coiled serpent at Mary's feet is poised to strike at San Francisco, a message of scorn. Could it be the ultimate message of revenge from an Inquisition victim?

I could understand it no other way. There was a second message in the painting. Behind San Francisco, on the right, is another image that has been added to the painting over the years.

It is the figure of Santa Teresa de Ávila, a Catholic mystic and nun who was the descendant of Jewish conversos. A cryptic golden line of tiny words is written upside down near her mouth in Spanish. It appears to mean "He who loves Doña listens to her handmaiden." "Doña" signifies the Virgin Mary, and the handmaiden is Santa Teresa.

Santa Teresa's philosophy was that true religion was found in the mind, not actions—the view of many Marranos who practiced one religion and believed another. Santa Teresa's paternal grandfather, Juan Sánchez de Toledo, was a converso tax collector and silk merchant who was tried by the Inquisition. He was accused of being a *"judaizante"*—a secretly practicing Jew—in 1485 in Toledo. Santa Teresa, who would later become a patron saint of Spain, was denounced to the Inquisition in 1574 by a princess who sent a copy of the nun's account of her life as proof that her visions and revelations were dangerous doctrines.

Santa Teresa ultimately was cleared by inquisitors, but much earlier her grandfather suffered a humiliating fate. These facts did not emerge in scholarly biographies of the Spanish saint until the 1940s. Juan Sánchez de Toledo and his children were forced to dress in the orange-and-yellow robes and coned hats of *sambenitos*. They marched through the streets of Toledo and its churches on seven successive Fridays, dodging stones flung at them by the crowds.

Today there is an expression in Spanish that survives from that time: *"llevar un sambenito."* It means "to carry a *sambenito"*—in effect, to bear some unmerited guilt or carry some undeserved shame. The expression is still used freely on Spanish television and in politics to accuse someone of telling falsehoods or smearing a person with lies.

NINETEEN

Below the Roses

Brussels, 2010

I often thought that I was not alone in my quixotic quest. How else to explain the medieval symbols that I started noticing in plain sight in my own house in France? One hangs in my master bedroom and I rarely notice it, though I sleep below it every night.

Several years ago, my brother-in-law Philippe—an avid amateur art collector—presented us with the gift of a little sixteenth-century oil painting of Santa Teresa by a Flemish painter, Andries Danielsz., from Antwerp. She is dressed in a nun's black veil and white habit, wreathed by red and white roses, ivory tulips, and lilies. A white parakeet hovers in a cloud near her upturned face, radiant with light. It was a portrait that, while arresting, was devoid of meaning for me. But when I delved into the history of the Spanish saint and her family, I began to look at Santa Teresa with completely fresh eyes. I was sure there was a message in the mystical wreath of roses and her right hand, which was raised upward in warning.

Roses, I learned, are an ancient symbol of silence. The Greek god Aphrodite gave a rose to her son, Eros, who then passed it to Harpocrates, the god of silence, to prevent gossip about his mother's sexual indiscretions. From this story, roses emerged in Western art and culture as a symbol of secrecy. The hosts of Roman banquets hung roses from ceilings to warn dinner guests to guard the secrets that were uttered there.

Whatever was heard in the room was guarded as a secret, *sub rosa* (Latin for "under the rose"), and should remain a secret. Could it be a message with a double meaning, a reference to Santa Teresa's own Marrano past? Ancient medieval symbols struggled to communicate.

I thought about this when I was dispatched in 2010 to Belgium to dig up a sinister secret. I was working on an ongoing news story about a bleak sex-abuse scandal in the tiny nation's long-powerful Catholic Church. The initial focus of the headlines was Roger Vangheluwe, bishop of Bruges and the longest-serving prelate in Belgium until he was forced to resign at age seventy-three. He did not appear at the news conference in April 2010 to announce his departure from a post that he had held for twenty-five years. So it was left to the newly named head of the Belgian Church, André-Joseph Léonard, to read the former bishop's brief statement.

"When I was not a bishop, and sometime later, I abused a boy. This has marked the victim mentally forever. The wound does not heal. Neither in me nor in the victim."

It was a staggering confession from the bishop who had zealously watched over his diocese from Bruges, a medieval city of canals called the "Venice of the North."

Bishop Vangheluwe had reigned over his flock like a father, sometimes short-tempered and sometimes generous and broad-minded. No detail was too small for his attention. He personally scolded parishes about reports that they had failed to pray the Apostles' Creed during mass. For relaxation at his sixteenth-century bishop's palace, he told an interviewer that he liked to pray in his garden and pick weeds. He didn't consider himself a rebel, but Bishop Vangheluwe personally pushed the Vatican in 2002 to allow women to be ordained deacons in a continent with a critical shortage of priests.

When he was appointed bishop at age forty-eight, Roger Vangheluwe was a handsome and charismatic Clark Kent of a figure with a square jaw and high energy. He easily shifted from playing the role of a seminary professor, whose specialties had been math, Christian theology, and biblical languages, to Church administration. Every year on the annual feast day of the Ascension, he marched in the procession of the Relic of the Holy Blood, carrying the bars of a gilded pallet on his shoulders and wearing a bishop's miter and handmade robes of Belgian lace.

The twelfth-century Relic of the Holy Blood is contained in a golden vial, sealed in red wax, and never opened. It was brought to Bruges after the Second Crusade and since then has been venerated for containing the preserved blood of Christ, which according to legend was obtained by Joseph of Arimathea after washing the body of Jesus. The holy day, celebrated forty days after Easter to mark the ascension of Christ's body and spirit into heaven, is marked every year in Bruges with an elaborate procession of men dressed as medieval knights and crusaders. And on that day, believers await a miracle when the blood liquefies.

After the bishop's resignation, most of the top clergy shunned the procession a few weeks later, fearing jeers from spectators. A humble priest carried the precious vial instead of a bishop. And a group of marching altar boys was greatly reduced, another effort to reduce potential hostilities.

The bishop's statement revealed few details about the boy who was his victim or his age at the time of the abuse. But he did reveal a clue, making reference to "abusing a boy in my close entourage."

"Over the past decades," he added in the statement, "I asked for the forgiveness of him and his family. But the media storm of the past few weeks only reinforced his trauma. It was not tenable anymore. I regret what I did and offer my most sincere apologies to the victim, his family, all the Catholic community and society."

After the disgraced bishop resigned, he retreated to a Trappist monastery in Westvleteren, in the west of Belgium, secure from criminal prosecution. Church officials said he could not be prosecuted because the victim and his family had not reported the abuse within the nation's statute of limitations, which is ten years after the victim turns eighteen.

So little was known about the victim that my colleague in Brussels, Stephen Castle, and I were assigned to search for him to understand why the silence held for so many years. Had he tried to alert Church authorities and been ignored?

I noticed that religion blogs from the United States were debating whether the boy was an older teen, a victim of what they called ephebophilia, sexual abuse of teenage boys. Their argument was that this abuse was more typical in the priesthood and that, in fact, pedophilia is actually rare. It seemed to me that some were poised to blame the victim for the abuse—a twisted logic that suggested both the bishop and his victim bore responsibility for what happened.

To find the silent victim, I tried all of the standard reporting techniques. I interviewed local priests and therapists. I contacted prosecutors and lawyers on the case, along with representatives of a new victims' group that emerged after a sudden flurry of more than 475 sexual abuse complaints were filed about priests after the bishop's highly public downfall. I had no name, just the quest to talk to him in order to understand why he kept his secret—a pattern that my family had also followed for their own reasons.

One priest told me he had communicated with the victim years earlier, through an intermediary who shielded his name. Another person gave me clues to his last name and his occupation as a hotel owner and artist. My colleague sifted through the mountain of facts we were accumulating, finally digging up the name of the rural bed-and-breakfast. I sent an e-mail to that address with a long letter explaining what we were doing, and asking to meet with him. Still silence.

On a hot summer afternoon in July, Stephen and I decided to seek out the victim. We rented a car and drove into the heart of West Flanders, rumbling past farms and flat, low-lying polder landscapes, enclosed by banks or dikes. We called his telephone number many times in advance of our arrival, but no one ever answered.

Eventually we ended up on a two-lane country road next to a sloping brick farmhouse perched not far from where two small rivers came together. Across a little pathway, goats grazed in a pasture under a blistering sun, which cast shadows from an enormous wooden sculpture of a primitive figure.

We walked past a dovecote, fluttering with pigeons, to the front door of the farmhouse. There we were greeted by another wood carving, about waist high and bleached by the sun to a coffee color. It was an image of a man, arms upraised, tilting in rage. The chest was slashed with a crosshatch of deep cuts, and the wide mouth and sharp teeth shaped a silent scream.

"This feels very welcoming," I said to Stephen.

"Quite cheerful," he replied in his dry British style.

I knocked at the door, tense in wait. A woman opened the

door and greeted us politely. We explained who we were and that we were trying to find a particular person for our reporting. To our surprise, she invited us into her living room and sent one of her three boys to fetch their father, who was swimming in the family pool.

Marc Vangheluwe entered the living room, still toweling himself dry. He was a slender man of forty-two, tanned from a recent vacation, with sun-bleached hair and gold spectacles. There was something fragile in the way he talked and sized up the two foreigners in front of him. He had the look of a man who had not lived life so much as endured it.

We explained again that we had tried to reach him without success and asked him for an interview. His English was shaky and our Flemish was nonexistent.

"Are you Roger Vangheluwe's nephew?"

"Yes."

"We are writing a story about the sexual abuse scandal to understand what happened, to understand why there was silence for so long."

"I don't know you, and it's hard for me to explain this in English to an outsider. It's not that it's hard to talk about. I'm just scared to talk because the Church has power. Ten years ago if I had talked about this, people would have put me away and said I was crazy."

"Why now?"

"It was a process."

We were alone now on a tour of a cluttered studio and his

farmhouse, lined with paintings. The couches in his living room had been vacated by his sons, who were sprawling among pillows when we arrived. His wife had also moved to another room, perhaps uncomfortable with his story or our presence or both.

He was reserved with us, a reflection of our lack of a shared language to speak with fluency and his almost child-like shyness. His answers were spare, and I struggled to think of a way to break the wall. I half expected him to usher us out the door. But he was far too polite to do this—or maybe he needed to talk.

Then I flashed on an idea: his art. Just as with medieval works of repressed Jewish conversos, a wretched, long-hidden story permeated his hand-carved sculptures and paintings.

On the walls of his house, I quickly scanned his stark, realistic paintings. One was a framework of porcelain plates and dishes, stacked askew, in individual compartments. There was a colorful landscape of tidy sloping churches with their doors closed. Churches with mutated towers. Boxes stacked by churches.

"What do these mean?" I asked, pointing to the paintings. "Boxes seem to be a recurring theme."

"For me it means a prison. Or maybe, it's a present as well. I give you something."

"And what about the wood sculptures, which seem to be screaming? What do they mean?"

"I do it with my eyes closed and that is the result. It's something inside me that does it. I follow my inner thoughts."

"I saw that you made a video posted online that shows a boy being pressed down in a box by a mattress. I think I got your message."

"Yes." Marc finally laughed. "A boy in a box."

By the time we said good-bye, we knew that Marc's abuse had lasted about ten years, from the age of eight, and that his father had confronted his brother, the bishop, when the boy turned eighteen. Later, more details would emerge from others, about a holy card that the Church circulated that enraged him. It was passed out to young teens making their confirmation, including the bishop's niece, and it contained a quote from the bishop extolling the joys of childhood.

We left the farmhouse and headed for the nineteenth-century Trappist abbey of Saint Sixtus of Westvleteren, not far from the medieval city of Ypres. Stephen had been there years before, when he worked for a British newspaper, and had written a story about the monks and their fabled beer, supposedly one of the best in the world and sold only from the monastery or reserved through a special "beer phone."

The monks defied all standard business models, shunning advertising for their beer and maintaining the philosophy: "We are not brewers. We are monks. We brew beer to afford being monks."

They also kept the vow of silence among themselves and were extraordinarily discreet, shunning most interview requests about the production of their storied beers, West-vleteren Blond, Westvleteren 8, and Westvleteren 12. Yet the brothers had faced a media storm by accepting the disgraced ex-bishop Roger Vangheluwe into their monastery. It was not without internal debate and disagreement that he was allowed to join their Spartan, carefully proscribed life. Prayer dominated their routine; they gathered seven times a day, starting with three-thirty a.m. vigils, continuing through seven a.m. lauds and eight-thirty a.m. mass, and finishing at seven-thirty p.m. for compline.

We sought an interview with a handwritten note for Roger Vangheluwe, delivered to a layman who acted as spokes-man for the twenty-four brothers in the monastery, three of them aging friars who attended services in wheelchairs. I was not surprised when we were told the ex-bishop was abiding by an agreement with the conference of bishops to shun interviews.

But I remembered from another story that I had written about monks in South Dakota that it was possible for the pub-lic to attend vespers after five p.m., a tradition that many dif-ferent orders share. So it was that Stephen and I took a place in the hard pews. I caught my breath when I saw the ex-bishop, who stood out among the monks in a homespun black-and-white robe and sandals. He no longer exuded power. He was a stooped figure in gray trousers, a short-sleeved shirt, and sandals. He held a prayer book in his hands, turned to Psalm 99, and chanted in a whisper from a back row.

I turned away from the old man. For a few minutes, I closed my eyes and savored the hypnotic chants of the monks who transported me to the cobblestone of Arcos, watching a *saeta* singer sway before a jeweled Virgin Mary.

Among the Trappist brothers, there is a tradition of soul searching called *lectio divina*, a heart-to-heart conversation with God. The idea is to read very slowly, searching for something fundamental, then pause. "You read again what has touched you," according to the monks, "you associate quietly, you consider what it has touched in you and what your answer might be. You taste and chew the fragment until you feel you squeezed out the nutrients."

The old monks call it *ruminatio*, like cows grazing on the grass. I wondered what the ex-bishop was finding to ruminate on in Psalm 99, which begins, "The Lord reigns, let the nations tremble," and warns that "the King is mighty, he loves justice."

The sun was pouring through the windows of the spare chapel, and some people started to leave, knowing that the last ten minutes were reserved for optional silent prayer.

I knew the Trappist brothers believe that quiet is one way for man to know himself and eventually God. But I found myself squirming in my seat, eager to flee the unbearable silence. The ex-bishop was praying in the quiet by the back wall. The unspoken tension in the air was repressive.

My head ached. My hands were numb and tingly. I could not erase the image of a screaming figure by the farmhouse, carved by the ex-bishop's nephew. And then began my own *ruminatio*. I replayed a conversation in my head with the rabbi who was the descendant of *chueta* conversos in Mallorca who told me: "Little by little, distance grows with the past or an angle of the past. Then comes a moment you say, 'I have nothing to do with this.'"

Was this the moment that I would break with the Church I grew up with? Is this how it feels to cut ties I thought would last for life? Silence.

The service ended. The ex-bishop studied his psalm and then filed out of the chapel in line with the other robed monks. The shuffle of their leather sandals was the only sound in the small, sacred place.

After he was gone, Stephen and I also left, passing through a leafy, well-tended garden and the monastery gift shop where we tried the best beer in the world.

"What did you think?" I asked Stephen as we headed toward the country road where our rental car was parked.

"I rather enjoyed it," he said. "It was really peaceful."

"I couldn't take it."

"Why was that?"

I paused, trying to figure it out. Why did I feel this way?

And then I realized the answer. It was that heavy feeling of the flow of silence through the centuries that trapped my ancestors in a hidden identity until the only way they could communicate was through double meanings, symbols, and hidden codes.

Had past and present changed all that much? In my mind, I kept seeing the image created by the ex-bishop's nephew, Marc Vangheluwe, propped upright by his farmhouse.

His sculpture of a screaming man, carved in splintering wood, was the texture of a medieval Spanish church door.

TWENTY

Synagogue de Notre Dame

Paris, 2010

In the same month in 1492 when all Jews were exiled from Spain, Christopher Columbus set sail for the Americas aboard the *Santa María*, the *Pinta*, and the *Niña* with a crew that included five Jews, freshly baptized into Christian conversos. One was a government translator, Yosef Ben Halevy Halvri, who changed his name to Luis de Torres and who spoke Hebrew, Portuguese, Aramaic, and Arabic—though for all his linguistic abilities ended up communicating in sign language when they arrived in the new land of Cuba. Some said he died in 1493, massacred by Indians after Columbus left thirty-nine members of the crew on the island when he returned to Spain. There are other, optimistic stories that he prospered on the island, assuming the role of royal agent, marrying the daughter of a local chief, and writing about his exploits, including a claim that on that first voyage to the New World, the conversos sang the Aramaic prayer of Kol Nidre for Yom Kippur, the Day of Atonement.

Flamenco experts have long theorized that it is the root of the plaintive *saetas* that linger in the air in Andalusian villages. The Kol Nidre dates to the sixth century, when the Visigoth king of Spain ordered Jews to convert or face death. Later, under Byzantine persecution in the ninth century and during the Spanish Inquisition, it gave solace to Spanish Jews when they gathered in secret to celebrate Yom Kippur. Prisoners in World War II camps also sang the melancholy music.

The prayer has long been controversial because it cancels religious vows between an individual and God. As a result, some eighth-century rabbinic authorities dismissed the Kol Nidre as a ridiculous practice, although for many Jews it is the most sacred prayer of the year. It was erased from nineteenth-century prayer books in many Western European communities, and Christians seized on the prayer to demonstrate that the oath of a Jew could not be trusted.

The words of the Kol Nidre are more dry and legalistic than the poetry of *saetas*. It is the music that carries the heartbreak. "By the authority of the heavenly court, and by the authority of this earthly court, with Divine consent and with the consent of this congregation, we hereby declare it permissible to pray with those who have transgressed."

The last word has been interpreted as a reference to

Spanish and Portuguese conversos who after 1492 returned to pray among openly Jewish communities in Amsterdam or Hamburg, where they were regarded with suspicion and resentment. They had lived as Jews and Christians, only to be scorned by both groups.

What happens when people lead dual lives, when they grow accustomed to hiding? The Kol Nidre was a second chance, offering those guarding secrets a chance to annul their religious oaths and come home.

I consider the *saeta* a chant tracing the journey of a soul in turmoil. The natural next step of the journey was sharing the prayer of the Kol Nidre. Could it have the power to transform me?

I had never heard the prayer before, never crossed the doors of a synagogue. The very idea of stepping inside unleashed disturbing dreams. In one, I was cornered in an outdoor party by an enormous, tawny lion from the pages of C. S. Lewis's Narnia fantasy that symbolized the son of God. The one woman next to me screamed to turn away to avoid his eyes. We both contracted in a heap, but I felt the breath of the lion, hovering over me, smelling my scent, and then turning away. Another man raced over. "You were arguing," he said.

I studied the listing for synagogues in Paris, searching for one with history and a Sephardic Jewish tradition. Browsing online, I discovered the perfect match for me: the Synagogue of Notre Dame, a few blocks from the river Seine. Most synagogues in the city are named for street locations, but in the case of the oldest synagogue in Paris, the official name is Synagogue of Nazareth. But people have stuck to habits, and the synagogue is often labeled informally for its quiet street in the neighborhood of the Marais, rue Notre-Dame-de-Nazareth.

I turned for advice on protocol to a friend and colleague, Dan, who was raised in a Jewish household in Montreal. He was rather cautious, urging me to call the synagogue ahead of Yom Kippur to seek a reservation or secure tickets for entry on a crowded holy day.

"Remember to bring your passport or identification," Dan said.

When I called to ask if I needed to bring identification to attend Yom Kippur services, the receptionist seemed startled.

"*Bien sûr*, the public is welcome," she said.

Even so, when I arrived there alone before sunset, metal barriers blocked both streets leading to the synagogue, which first opened in 1822 with permission from King Louis XVIII. French policemen kept vigil at both ends of the block—a legacy of modern politics and the past when the synagogue was attacked in October 1941 by French collaborators, who caused little damage. A plaque hangs in the synagogue in memory of one rabbi, Joseph Saks, and his wife, who were deported during the German occupation when the synagogue's neighbor was a Gestapo bureau.

Inside, the synagogue opened into a neo-Moorish sanctuary drenched with Oriental colors of turquoise and gold, white and crimson. Bright blue arched stained-glass windows marked the twelve tribes of Israel. White candles flickered in the prayer hall. I wasn't sure where to sit after I noticed that seats on the main floor were filled with men in prayer shawls and yarmulkes. Then I noticed women and children thundering up narrow wooden steps to three vast galleries that looked down toward the Ark, almost like theater seats.

Some of the families had been coming to these Yom Kippur services for four generations, their names marked on backs of seats in the women's gallery. I searched for one that wasn't claimed and then watched another familiar French ritual unfold. Women in chic dresses made their way slowly down the aisles, planting kisses among old friends in their wake.

The services were late, well past sundown. I noticed people repeatedly studying an enormous clock in the synagogue with the minute hand ticking toward eight p.m. The murmur of voices grew to a rumble, then hushed as two men entered and took two Torah scrolls from an Ark. Then they took their places on each side of a cantor and the three men—representing a *beth din,* or rabbinical court—began to pray.

The cantor's voice was a sweet tenor. As he chanted the Kol Nidre, I closed my eyes to let the melody wash over me, silencing the side of my brain that worried about meaning. A woman next to me hummed along, and by her a baby wailed. The cantor began on a falling note, lingering for two phases softly on the same prayer. The subdued opening is what masters of Catholic plainsong call pneuma—soul breath—a long sighing tone, falling to a lower note, rising again. Then the cantor repeated the prayer a third time in a chant of defiant ascents.

It was the powerful voice of Jewish history, tracing an arc of despair and hope. I know its echo on a silvery gray cobblestone lane in Arcos de la Frontera, a *saetero* rending the night with an anguished prayer.

When I was in Barcelona in El Call, Rabbi Ben Avraham—the Catholic schoolboy turned converso emissary—talked about knowing almost mystically when he was ready to break with his family's borrowed religion and identity. He described a moment when the soul simply heard the call. I listened to the Kol Nidre, which stirred something deep inside, essential and ancient. But so much stood in the way.

After the Kol Nidre was finished, the rabbi stood in the sanctuary to deliver an address. He spoke in French with an accent, and there was noise all around me. I found it difficult to understand him, until I heard the word "Inquisition" and felt the electric current that had struck me so many times in Arcos de la Frontera.

How strange that his message struck me like a sharp note. I stood up, moved toward the railing, and resisted the urge to beat my heart. That was much too Catholic.

The story he told was a perfect parable, the story of a historic meeting in 2004 when the chief rabbi of Israel, Yona Metzger, joined Spain's King Juan Carlos. They were marking the eight hundredth anniversary of the death of the

Jewish philosopher and physician Maimonides, who was from Córdoba.

The rabbi recounted how the chief rabbi gave the king an elegantly polished shofar, fitted with silver and engraved with a royal crown.

"What is the meaning of this?" the king asked, studying the horn, made from a ram and blown on the holy days of Rosh Hashanah and Yom Kippur.

"Five hundred years ago, when your great-great-grandfather King Ferdinand and Queen Isabella expelled my ancestors," the chief rabbi said, "many Jews remained in Spain by becoming Marranos, who behaved as Christians, yet remained Jews privately."

In 1492, he said, Ferdinand de Aguilar, a Marrano and the conductor of the Royal Orchestra in Barcelona, approached King Ferdinand to arrange a free public concert of wind instruments. The conductor chose the day that fell on the Jewish holiday of Rosh Hashanah. On that day, the composer displayed the shofar to the aristocrats and ministers in the front rows, ahead of the Marranos who sat behind them. The king and queen were entertained by a quaint instrument, but the conversos were touched, whispering the shofar blessings.

As he stood before King Juan Carlos in 2004, the chief rabbi said, "Now I can present this shofar to you because you are blessed with democracy. Now in Spain everyone can pray without fear."

When the rabbi in the Paris synagogue finished his story,

I looked around me. I am not sure how many people were touched by his message. But it made me think of another story I had heard, this one of a rebbe in the 1940s who advised a German student who was considering converting to Christianity to secure a place in a university. Then he heard the notes of a Kol Nidre prayer and reconsidered.

"Did God give you an answer?" the rebbe asked of the student, who started to weep.

"I forgot the question. I put all my attention on the path, and after a while I took so much pleasure in the journey that I forgot about the question."

"In that case," the rebbe said, "I would say that God gave you your answer."

TWENTY-ONE

Between the Voices

Paris, 2010

If God isn't real, then all the rest—the traditions, the rituals, the worship—are empty. In song I find a religion that gives solace.

Yet what should I pass on to the next generation, to my daughter, Claire, now fourteen? She was baptized, of course, at one week old, in a gauzy christening dress made by my aunt Marion; I didn't want to consign her to limbo. She attends the Catholic École de Notre Dame outside Paris, by the river Oise. The sisters of Notre Dame have long vanished. The school is so secular that when my daughter asked a school administrator if she needed to wear a veil for her First

Communion ceremony, the administrator regarded her with French horror.

"We don't do that here."

My mother, Carol, had made me a gauzy Communion veil with a lacy crown of fringe so high that it blocked out the girl behind me in our First Communion portrait. We took refuge in the rituals then, but they weren't holding for me anymore.

My daughter asked me why I don't take Communion on the very rare occasions that we attend mass. I told her I just don't feel comfortable doing it, and she accepted that without pressing for an explanation. When she and her classmates made their confirmation in the white robes of acolytes at a towering stone church painted by Matisse, parents were asked to stand next to them near the altar. Claire tipped her unlit candle toward mine and I lit the orange flame, marking a rite of passage into adulthood in the Church.

I have mixed feelings. I can live with my own ambivalence about the Church, but what do I pass along to her as a legacy, beyond my own doubts? I have tried to weave our past into casual conversations while we lived in Andalusia and when we returned every summer. In 2008, I gave her a novel called *Blood Secret*, about a high school freshman girl who is abandoned by her mother and moves in with her ninety-four-year-old grandmother in Albuquerque, New Mexico. There she wanders down a creaky stairway and discovers the proverbial heirloom-filled trunk in her grandmother's basement. It magically reveals the lives of ancestors who were Jews persecuted during the Spanish Inquisition and who reveal their lives in first-person tales.

How easy to have all the answers in one box. But the tale raised questions that I am wrestling with: the power of silence, the legacy of persecution, and the secrets passed through generations.

"You know, we have Jewish ancestors," I told my daughter when I gave her the paperback book. She started to read it, but abandoned it that summer for *Treasure Island*.

Her own Catholic school has done a better job of educating her about the Jewish faith than I have. She comes home with handouts from her world religion class with readings about Abraham and Moses, commandment tablets, and the twelve tribes of Israel. She is also studying Spanish in her school, attending language immersion camps in Spain for foreign students who mingle with Spanish students studying English. One summer, twins from New Jersey whose father was a Brazilian Jew befriended my daughter at the camp.

When we picked her up to head back to Arcos de la Frontera, she recounted tales of camp life. Then she told me about her new friend from New Jersey who had recently celebrated a bat mitzvah party.

"I wish we were Jews," she said almost wistfully.

"You know, you have Jewish ancestry," I said.

"No," she said. "I mean really Jewish."

Some rabbis who work with conversos talk about a feeling of *añoranza*, a yearning or longing to be whole, a universal quest. For Claire, it comes naturally. We have three countries, the United States, France, and Spain. Her Spanish mother is María José, our neighbor in Arcos de la Frontera, who has three sons. The youngest is Pablo.

When we left Spain for the summer to return to France, María José held Pablo in her arms, to say good-bye to Claire. I watched Pablo whisper in his mother's ear and we heard her say, *"Siempre."* Always. I knew he was asking if we would come back. If he asked me, I would give him the same answer his mother did.

At one point, I thought that science would give me concrete answers about my ancestors, tracking them home precisely through genetic clues. In Costa Rica, my paparazzo lawyer had churned up records of an assortment of Carvajals, though he could never follow the paper trail far enough to determine whether our family line was connected to the original Costa Rican settler, Antonio Carvajal, who arrived on one of the boats from the fourth voyage of Columbus.

One day, while digging through Mormon archives of baptismal records from Costa Rica, I found marriage records in 1880 for my great-great-grandfather José Carvajal. I studied the tight writing of the notary that declared the marriage of José Carvajal to Petronilla Alvarado, who would later have eleven children, nineteen grandchildren, and twenty-six great-grandchildren.

The cursive handwriting was so cramped that it was difficult to make out the text. The names of Petronilla's parents were on the form, listing her as an *hija legítima*, a legitimate

daughter. Then I noticed the name of María Carvajal, the
mother of my great great-grandfather. But she was the only
one listed on his side, and there was no reference to a father.

I studied the reference again, enlarging the text. Then
I noticed two words between the lines that surprised me. I
clasped my forehead in disbelief. This was the moment in
genealogy research that some politely call a "surprise negative" or a "nonpaternal event." It means a break in ancestry—
somewhere in the family tree a surname doesn't match or a
genetic sample or profile differs from the rest of the group.

In this case, two words explained it: *hijo natural*—illegiti-
mate son. My great-great-grandfather had obviously taken his
mother's family name, Carvajal. After endless hours searching for his birth or baptismal records, I turned up nothing,
including adoption records. My father's male line stretched
before me—an endless, open mystery. I could not find a marriage record for his mother.

There was no oracle to consult. Cecilia, my cousin who
was the storekeeper of family lore, was long dead. My father
remembered hearing whispers about something, but he
didn't know the details. I always regretted that I didn't have a
trunk of dusty letters to browse through for clues. But I had
saved dozens of letters that Cecilia had sent me over the years.
They were all postmarked Costa Rica, a stack of flimsy little
envelopes, always with a border of red, white, and blue.

I went through each one carefully. They offered a wealth
of routine information about her health, Mexican vacations,
eye surgeries, rainstorms, diabetes, the death of her little

mutt, Cassiopeia, her son's heart problems. But then I came across a letter from May 2003. It was written in blue ink in her girlish hand. Jammed between family news was an offhand comment about a nugget of family history. I obviously did not bother to read between the lines when I first received the letter.

"Well, listen to this intrigue," she wrote. "Your great-great-grandfather, José Carvajal, was a Carvajal and a Rodríguez. The Carvajal name was that of his mother. José Carvajal fought with his father and never wanted to use his name. For that we are all Carvajals."

But who was his father and who were this new line of relatives through the centuries whom we knew absolutely nothing about?

When I approached my uncle in Costa Rica, Roy Carvajal, the mystery deepened. I had it on his word that the spelling of the name was "Rodrigues." A different story, another detour. This could be true or not in a local oral tradition inclined to some embroidery.

"The history that you want was told to me by Aunt Luz and it is the truth," he wrote to me. "It seems that he was the son of a rancher and his mother married a Carvajal who recognized him as their son. That is the history I was told and a *señora* I knew also told me the same story and I believe it is certain because she had nothing to do with the Carvajal family."

My cousin Javier added another layer to the version when he told me what his grandmother, my great-aunt Luz, had told him: "We have Jewish ancestors on two sides of the family, on the Carvajal side of our great-grandfather and on the maternal side of his wife, Pérez. Our great-grandfather used to visit the house of a rabbi. More than that, I don't know any more about our Jewish roots."

TWENTY-TWO

River's End

Bay of Cádiz, 2008

I could barely hear my aunt Ligia Carvajal on the telephone line when she summoned me to meet her in Cádiz, the port city where the Guadalete River flows from Arcos de la Frontera into the immense blue waters of the Bay of Cádiz.

"You are where exactly?"

"I am leaving for a voyage on a Spanish navy ship."

"What? Are you kidding?"

Her voice faded to an unintelligible crackle and she strained to hear mine. She is the daughter from my grandfather's third marriage, his last child, about ten years older than I. Many times I have pressed her for information about

~~~

our family's past, though her information was usually sketchy. I had also asked her about the Rodríguez line, but she had steered me to another relative.

And now, she was calling me from Spain; she had recently settled in Madrid. Her appearance in the port of Cádiz on a Spanish navy vessel was not what I expected.

I shouted questions into my mobile telephone, waving it in circles to get better reception on the old rock of Arcos. But I couldn't hear her explanation about what she was doing aboard a Spanish navy training ship.

"Meet me at three on Saturday. The ship's name is *Juan Sebastián de Elcano*, like the explorer. Call you later."

When my husband and I drove into Cádiz two days later, I wasn't quite sure what we would find in the historic city where adventurers, exiles, and some of my ancestors took flight and scattered around the world. I had never heard of the ship. So I was startled when I caught my first glimpse of the *Elcano*.

It was a pure-white steel schooner with four enormous masts, moving briskly by engine power through the painfully blue bay on a hot, windless July afternoon.

A drift of a yellow-and-red Spanish flag fluttered in the sky. In the distance I could see a tiny golden image of a woman pressing forward from the prow and the coat of arms of Spanish explorer Juan Sebastián Elcano, captain of Ferdinand Magellan's last exploratory voyage. It also carried his motto, bestowed by King Charles I of Spain: *"Primus Circumdedisti Me,"* or "You Circumnavigated Me First."

At 370 feet long, the *Elcano* is the third-largest tall sailing ship in the world, built more than eighty years ago, in 1927, in Cádiz. As it breezed close to port, I could see Aunt Ligia in dark sunglasses, surrounded by mostly men in crisp navy whites, and an older officer with a stiff-brimmed cap and a video camera.

The ship is a floating academy for six-month cruises to train the Spanish navy's midshipmen. It also doubles as a seafaring embassy, calling into port in foreign countries in many of its former colonies like Costa Rica or Panama, but also docking in Istanbul, Venice, London, Hamburg, Lisbon, and St. Petersburg. After every cruise, the *Elcano* returns to Cádiz in July in time for the festival of La Virgen del Carmen.

For this particular cruise, the commander was Javier Romero Caramelo, who acted as a captain and statesman, hosting elegant diplomatic parties aboard the ship around the world and spreading goodwill for the Spanish government.

The *Elcano* also plays an informal role as something of an international love boat. "There are people who have come here to see young sailors with intentions of making connections," Commander Caramelo said in a whimsical interview with a reporter from the newspaper *El País*, who was also on board with my aunt. "And I do have friends who married women from other countries who they met on trips with the *Elcano*."

That would have been the moment for Commander Caramelo, who yearns to have lived and sailed in the sixteenth century, to mention my aunt Ligia. But he was too discreet.

Or perhaps it was because, as he said in his interview, "all sailors are a little romantic."

The commander had invited Aunt Ligia aboard the *Elcano* for part of the voyage because of her own relentless journey that started on the white ship and spanned forty years, a dozen countries, and two broken marriages.

Long ago, when Aunt Ligia was fourteen, and willowy and tall for her age, she attended a glittering party aboard the *Elcano*, which was docked in Costa Rica. She was chaperoned by her mother, among all the Spanish midshipmen and Costa Rican and Spanish diplomats. Tables were set with white linen silver candelabras. Men in dress uniforms and gloves served platters of seafood and Spanish wine. That's when she saw José Luis among the men in white, a towering, handsome midshipman with blue-gray eyes.

I didn't remember this story when I scanned the ship for Aunt Ligia, waiting for her to reach the dock, crowded with families of returning sailors. She insisted she told me the tale when I moved to Costa Rica in the 1980s for a summer immersion program in Spanish in the capital city of San José. Too much life had intervened and I had forgotten the story, the kind you share with each other on lazy days by the beach at sunset on the Pacific or staying up late talking till tumblers of rum and Coke—our drink of choice in those days—emptied. Aunt Ligia is another family wanderer who consumes life in great gulps. Over the course of her life she changed professions from dentist to Third World aid advisor, and some days she is living in Costa Rica or sending me e-mails from Equatorial Guinea, Indonesia, or Afghanistan. She also calls Madrid home.

My aunt is a serenely beautiful woman, inside and out, with enormous amber-brown eyes, honey-blond hair, and a musical laugh that draws people around her. She liked to think of herself as a gypsy, a little wild and untamed, though the years had a way of changing that.

She is a believer in the theory of waves, that civilizations rise and fall and ebb, as do relationships. When my wave first washed toward her, she was divorced from a Panamanian dentist and married to a much older American military advisor who had retired to Costa Rica. Then through the years he drifted away, corresponding with an old high school girl-friend in Kentucky who drew him away from my aunt, back to his past.

As the marriage receded, Aunt Ligia started to look back in another direction to Spain and the midshipman named José Luis. Their lives had ebbed and flowed for more than forty years, each married to someone else, each with their own children.

When they were young, Aunt Ligia and José Luis tried to forge a connection after meeting on the *Elcano*. At age fifteen, Aunt Ligia traveled with her mother to Spain to meet José Luis's parents. But his mother didn't approve, deeply unimpressed with Aunt Ligia's lack of cooking and sewing skills.

"I was raised to study," Aunt Ligia recalled. "She couldn't accept it."

They saw each other again aboard the *Elcano*, when Aunt Ligia sold her sweet-sixteen pearls to fly to Panama to meet José Luis at the port, always with her mother in tow. Then the relationship sputtered, unable to survive the barriers of disapproving parents, jobs, and geography.

Four decades later, with her second marriage crumbling, Aunt Ligia took a trip to Madrid to visit a friend. As they strolled past the military offices of the Spanish navy, she abruptly decided to seek help there to locate José Luis. They wouldn't give out private information, but they accepted her business card and promised to mail it along.

That is how the wave swept her back to Spain. Months later he contacted her in Costa Rica. She flew to Madrid and stayed, though they had no idea if this time their relationship would endure.

The story of their unrequited forty-year romance spread among the Spanish navy elite who played golf together and shared dinners and cards. The commander called to extend an invitation to José Luis and Aunt Ligia for a voyage on the *Elcano* to savor the ending, or rather the beginning, of a four-decade-old romance.

When I saw José Luis for the first time aboard the ship, he was no longer a young midshipman, but was wearing a white dress uniform, panning a video camera over the masts of the *Elcano*. Then he saluted Commander Caramelo and started marching down the gangway.

Later José Luis would tell me that he couldn't believe it when he received Aunt Ligia's card. He immediately responded with an e-mail message. Days passed without an answer, but time was nothing. He had been waiting forty years. Then a note came back, and more correspondence followed.

"I never gave up," José Luis said, telling a story that by now he had recounted to many in the Spanish navy, who were charmed by the enduring romance linked to the ship and the sea.

But they didn't know about the other tale of our family, which had lasted far longer. I thought about our past as we stood together, Aunt Ligia and I, beside the magnificent pure-white *Elcano*. There was not a drift of wind to ease the heat from a fiery sun. I studied the towering masts of the tall ship, marveling that the Carvajals had come back to the beginning, at the invitation of the Spanish Royal Navy.

I gazed at the vast blue Bay of Cádiz, where the forgetting river of the Guadalete spilled to its end, where Columbus set sail on his fourth and final voyage that would take him to Costa Rica.

For a few moments, on dry land, I savored the wave washing over me.

TWENTY-THREE

Cry of the Stones

Palma, Mallorca, Spain, May 2011

"Shalom!" So began the brief message from Israel, a note from Michael Freund, the New Yorker tending descendants of converso Jews through his educational organization, Shavei Israel. "I just want you to know about a special event on the island of Mallorca. This will be historic."

Whenever anyone makes that promise to me, my natural reaction is to steel myself, always doubting. But still I was intrigued when I heard Michael's description of a small group of Orthodox rabbis from Israel bound for Mallorca's port city, Palma, in the spring of 2011 to say a prayer for the dead during a special memorial, centuries overdue.

The May anniversary was approaching of an auto-da-fé

held on a hillside overlooking Palma in 1691. It was an elaborate, public church ritual that started with a mass, a public procession of accused heretics, and ultimately execution by burning at the stake. This dark legacy of the *cremadissa*—mass burning—is shameful history that the Balearic regional government had surprisingly agreed to confront. Catholic converts who secretly practiced their forbidden religion during the Inquisition were burned in Plaza Gomila in a "bonfire of the Jews," and their descendants, labeled *chuetas*, were scorned for generations, through the twentieth century.

Mallorca, largely isolated until the tourist boom reached it and the other Balearic Islands in the late 1960s, developed into a wary preserve for the converso descendants who protected themselves by making public professions of Catholic faith, marching in brotherhoods for Easter processions, and carving crucifixes in stone outside their homes in the warren of the island's old Jewish quarter. Extensive family trees show descendants are intertwined because they married among themselves, shunned as marriage material by old Christian families preferring *limpieza de sangre*, clean blood.

With the arrival of floods of tourists from different countries, the island culture started to change, but a modest synagogue did not open in the center of Mallorca until the 1970s and remains so low-key that some local taxi drivers say they have never heard of Comunitat Israelita de Mallorca, which is set back on a side street and protected by a special parking barrier.

I called local Spanish politicians and asked if something truly historic was about to happen.

"We think we are the first in Spain," an advisor to the regional president of the Balearic Islands told me. "But you'd better check."

They weren't prepared to make an apology precisely, he told me, but to express regrets for the island's brutal history when four autos-da-fé were staged on the edge of the city and a total of eighty-two people were ultimately executed for secretly observing Judaism.

"We weren't there then, so we can't apologize for what others did," he explained.

Most of the converso Jews escaped the worst punishment by repenting and accepting Christianity. For their contrition, they were hanged and their bodies cast in a bonfire. But three people refused to convert and were burned alive at the stake: a brother and a sister, Raphael Benito Terongí and Catalina Terongí, and a secret rabbi, Raphael Valls, a soap and oil merchant who had led the clandestine religious activities. It was Rabbi Valls who organized an attempt to escape the "Golden Island" in March 1688 with dozens of other wealthy conversos in a hired English vessel bound for Amsterdam, but a fierce storm forced them back.

On their return, the news of their flight and secret religious activities spread quickly. The brother-in-law of Raphael Valls, who had also tried to flee, confessed the names of all the families, explaining that they tried to leave because they feared false accusations against them would be lodged with the Inquisition. Children as young as eleven were arrested and the adults were imprisoned for almost five years in the Bellver Castle, which has loomed over the city's port in the Mediterranean for seven hundred years. There on a hillside outside their prison, they were executed with a Jesuit eyewitness, Francisco Garau, proclaiming, "They have been saved from the perils of the water only to perish in the fire."

What intrigued me about the *chuetas* was that those executions became part of the living history of Palma, scarring the lives of descendants well into the twentieth century. The Inquisition meted out penalties intended to last two generations, applying to children and grandchildren of the condemned. They could not hold public offices, serve as priests, or marry persons other than *chuetas*. Instead the daily humiliations carried on for many more generations into modern times.

When Michael described the planned memorial to me, he mentioned a haunting detail that finally drove me to book a ticket from Paris to Palma.

"There's an old Catholic church in Palma that was built above the remains of the city's oldest synagogue," he said. "Some of the old stones of the synagogue are smooth and discolored by the foundation because *chueta* descendants used to trace their hands along it and kiss their fingers."

Rarely do visitors come to this port city like these tourists in dark suits from Israel who arrived in bright sunshine in May and mingled, looking out of place, among cruise passengers in shorts and tennis shoes from enormous Italian ships docked in the port.

The group from Israel had mapped out their plans: touch the smooth sandstone foundation of the fourteenth-century synagogue turned into the Roman Catholic church of Nuestra Señora de Montisión. Recite a long-delayed fifteenth-century prayer for the victims of the Inquisition.

When I joined the Israeli visitors on a walk through the *casco antiguo*, the old quarter of Palma, the handful of Orthodox rabbis in dark suits turned heads. One visitor was Joseph Wallis, a burly man in his sixties who wore a black suit, crisp white shirt, and a dark yarmulke, and was sweating in the heat. His silver beard was carefully trimmed and when he spoke to others in Hebrew, I heard gravelly traces of a Bronx accent. The other was Rabbi Nissan Ben Avraham, whom I had met earlier in a Barcelona bookstore and who was raised Catholic in Mallorca and later converted, to the dismay of his *chueta* father, a local shopkeeper.

Centuries ago their relatives had faced death together during the 1691 auto-da-fé. Rabbi Ben Avraham's ancestor, Catalina Terongí, was burned alive next to Rabbi Wallis's ancestor, Rafael Valls. She urged him, according to Inquisition records, to ignore the flames, to hold on to his faith.

For Rabbi Wallis, this visit to Mallorca was a homecoming, the closing of a circle of defiance. His father, a Holocaust survivor, always remembered the name of Rafael Valls, he said, because it topped a list of relatives contained in an old family Bible that was passed down for generations but vanished during World War II. The spelling of his family name changed to Wallis, he said, as they moved to new countries in the East.

As we walked together through Palma, we talked about his distant Spanish ancestor and the gift that he believes Raphael Valls passed on to his descendants, including Rabbi Wallis's father, who survived imprisonment in the Dachau camp.

"I asked my father how he survived," he said. "They suffered so much. What gave them strength? I think it was our roots going back to Raphael Valls that gave us the willpower to remain and pursue our tradition."

On his mother's side they were just as defiant. Her father, an ultra-Orthodox rabbi from Hungary, died in a personal act of rebellion, he recalled.

"The Nazis called the Jews to form a circle and they ordered my grandfather to step forward," he said. "'In a few hours you will be freed,' a Nazi told my grandfather. 'But if you want to live, take a bite of this pork.' When he refused, the Nazi took out his resolver and screamed: 'If you eat this, you can go home. If not, die like a dog.' My grandfather just shook his head and the Nazi pulled the trigger and he fell to the ground dead. It was the last day before the war ended."

His family history reminded me of dramatic stories that I read as a child about martyrs and saints who made stark choices between life and death. Perhaps some of the legends about the saints amounted to mythmaking. My family had chosen another path. So had generations of *chuetas* in Palma who ate the pork, who carried the cross, who lived dual lives in order to survive and avoid the fire. Even the stalwart Rabbi Valls had tried to flee with his wife, who was also executed.

I thought about this as I walked with Rabbi Wallis toward the church of Nuestra Señora de Montesión, through twisting lanes of salmon-colored houses with green shutters, which are a common sight in the *casco antiguo*—an old symbol from the Muslims, who believed that green represented life and nature.

"The Valls," he mused, "didn't give up. My father came from a family that just didn't give up."

He was their legacy. When we reached the baroque seventeenth-century portal of the church, he fell silent. I studied the elaborate entry of pillars and pilasters with columns wrapped with stone flowers and fruits. On either side stand statues of the first Jesuit saints, the missionary Francis Xavier and Ignatius of Loyola, who founded the Jesuit order and clashed with the Inquisition. He was denounced for his peculiar dress and accused of belonging to the sect of the Illuminati. Above the burgundy doors, carved in stone, is the inscription DILIGIT DOMINUS PORTAS SION, "The Lord Loves the Gates of Zion."

But our group ignored the opulent entrance. Rabbi Ben Avraham pointed instead toward a bare wall of the church in the shadows of a narrow alley, Carrer del Vent. The street of the wind. In the darkness, we could all see a ragged line of vanilla stones, remnants of a synagogue. Not even the stones were spared, I thought, as I watched each rabbi touch the wall in silence.

I also traced the rough texture with my fingers, willing myself back in time. Forgetting is the injustice, I thought, and then dropped my hand. It was no surprise, perhaps, that the church bells began to toll.

Later I would trail the rabbis along the street where the monastery of Santo Domingo displayed orange-and-yellow *sambenito* costumes that the victims were forced to wear on their march to the auto-da-fé. The robes were draped there for centuries on public exhibition, another Inquisition punishment that intensified the isolation and segregation of *chuetas* because each robe carried a family's name. Until 1820, the robes hung there. But one day that year, a group of *chuetas* attacked the church and burned the *sam-benitos*.

Now, of course, the biggest danger is forgetting. Many of the people with those fifteen names gathered for the public memorial for the Jewish victims of the Inquisition in the courtyard of a government building near a church. Its bells thundered so loudly during the ceremony that it was as if they had joined in a prayer for the dead.

"Let suffering speak because this is the beginning of all truth," said Aina Aguiló Bennassar, a *chueta* descendant.

As the ceremony ended at twilight, I lingered in the courtyard to talk to some of the *chuetas* who still seemed amazed by the sympathetic attention. Many of their last names were read aloud by Rabbi Ben Avraham during the ceremony as he intoned the names of the dead from 1691.

In the back rows, I could see Bernat Pomar, a retired concert violinist and music teacher, nodding at the mention of Catalina Pomar, who was executed at the age of seventy-one. Then came another name, Raphael Agustín Pomar, thirty-nine. The night before, Bernat had celebrated a small party with Rabbi Wallis and Rabbi Ben Avraham to mark his conversion to Judaism. At age seventy-eight, he had undergone circumcision and confided his secret to his grown children only that week, although he had been thinking about conversion and studying for years. He did not want them to feel forced to follow his example.

"There was fear, always fear," said Bernat, who explained to me why it took so long to tell his own family. "Behind the curtains, we were afraid. *Chuetas* are special because the community of Mallorca shaped us."

Later I met Bernat Aguiló Siquier, a government official in a suit and tie, who was eager to talk. For the first time, he pointed out, the *chuetas* were being publicly recognized by a government institution. Now schoolchildren are baffled when his son tells them that he is a *chueta*, he said. But he remembers when the name provoked schoolyard taunts and his grandfather was restricted to sitting in a special pew in a Catholic church, where he was required to wear a yellow jacket, the mark of the family's shame.

"We always knew that we were descended from people who died at the gallows for their religious beliefs and suffered from the persecution of the Inquisition," he said. "That just made me stronger."

With the insular nature of the island, many *chuetas* could trace their families back for hundreds of years in neatly lettered genealogical trees that showed how they had married among themselves, weaving together the fifteen family names. But it was a complicated tradition. Unlike Jews who trace their religious heritage on the maternal line, *chuetas* were marked by their names on the paternal line.

"*Chuetas* weren't the only ones who married among themselves," Bernat said. "All of the Mallorcans married by class. *Chuetas* married among themselves until the 1950s and the aristocrats did the same thing until the 1970s.

"So what is the characteristic of the *chuetas*? For me, it's the stigma," he said. "Our name was an insult. Marrying among ourselves was an act of a pariah group—contaminated by their transgressions."

In the haberdashery of Rabbi Ben Avraham's family, there is an elaborate family tree of green and blue that dates back five hundred years and is stored in the upstairs stockroom. The family store, Angela—which sells an assortment of ribbons, socks, embroidery thread, and Spanish fans—has evolved with the tree, its name changing with each new generation of owners of the same store that dates back to the seventeenth century.

The same familiar *chueta* names are spread along the family branches, with more than 560 people rising from the roots. I noticed that Israel Wiesel, a rabbi with the group from Israel and a judge for an ultra-Orthodox court, studied this chart closely, tracing the common patterns of families named Pomar, Fuster, Piña, Terongí, and Rabbi Ben Avraham's own birth name, Aguiló. I later learned Rabbi Wiesel had a discreet legal mission: to gather information to submit to other judges on his court to decide whether converso descendants are indeed Jews despite centuries of persecution and discrimination that forced them to convert to survive.

Rabbi Wiesel was an unlikely genealogical detective in his stiff black hat and spectacles, but he had come searching for evidence of the past in the present. Unlike other Marranos who scattered, the *chuetas* were almost like hothouse flowers who had remained on the island for centuries, consistently marrying among themselves, and offering research possibilities to scientists who studied the patterns of their DNA. It was much easier, ultimately, for the rabbinical court in Israel to determine a few months later that the *chuetas* were Jews on the basis of the evidence that Rabbi Wiesel gathered for a decision that he called "headline ruling."

"We can't say that each and every member of the *chueta* community has the faith," he explained to me later in a telephone call from Israel. "Over the last two generations there has been some intermarriage, but by and large if a community has remained a pure line of history for the last seven hundred years, despite oppression and persecution, then they are Jews."

But they did not apply the same pure line of history to Catholic descendants of Jews in Spain, Portugal, and the United States because the chances were that the line was broken among the generations through marriage to others. Still, the court had uncovered clear patterns that families in these far-flung countries had passed on rituals even if they often didn't understand their meanings.

"There are millions of people in Central and South America who have a line of descent from the Marranos," he told me. "Hundreds have come to our court to convert, from Brazil, Colombia, Argentina, Chile, Venezuela, Mexico, Costa Rica. We have many.

"We hear the same stories from people who come to convert. They all kept one sort of custom, at least one Jewish custom from father to son that they held on to very strongly.

"For example, they only ate chicken that was strictly slaughtered. Some covered the mirrors when someone died. Some were buried facing Jerusalem. Each family kept a certain custom."

Schulamith Chava Halevy, the Hebrew University researcher mentioned earlier, collected similar stories and anecdotes about unique rituals from converso descendants, of psalms frequently read in connection with death before and after burial, but without the usual Christian prayers.

The rabbi had offered me tantalizing advice. Did my family guard a custom? Perhaps it was another ritual lost to the forgetting river. I had tried to inhabit the world of my ancestors, but at some point I had to accept that they were unknowable. Some aspects of their story were simply impenetrable.

I wondered what drove them, exactly, to board a sailing ship to flee Spain from the Bay of Cádiz. Did they have regrets or find a sense of home? Did they expect new generations to reclaim their religion?

My contemporary answer came from the elderly violinist Bernat Pomar, who made peace with the contradictions of his life and his family through his music. His compact disc *Suite de Danses de Mallorca* explored wildly incongruous themes, from tolerance and Israel to flamenco beats and the dances of Mallorca.

We met twice. Each time I pressed him with questions to understand why he converted so late in life. When he was young, he recalled, there was only the Catholic Church. His parents never talked about their *chueta* background, and he remembered learning about the origins of his name from a book published decades ago.

"I figured it out," he said, staring into a cup of coffee, cars roaring in the street near the terrace where we sat. "No one told me. I didn't ask about it, because you did not ask about these things.

"I didn't know anything. I didn't know who we were. I always felt inferior."

When Franco started to loosen restrictions on religion in the late 1960s, Bernat believed that it was the moment to return. But he couldn't.

"A *chueta* could not ask about this. It's a very strange thing. Now I should be able to explain this, but I can't," he said.

I tried to probe further, but there was so much left unsaid in his conversation. His sentences were full of pauses and detours. It seemed easier for him to communicate through his violin, emotions that lingered in bittersweet notes. He had passed this legacy on to many talented violinists who learned to play at age three through his special system, El Meu Violí. Bernat developed a technique to teach them traditional Mallorcan songs by reading the symbols of animal drawings and icons. And they rewarded him in turn by treating him like a grandfather. It wasn't hard: he had a warm and thoughtful quality, even though sometimes he found it difficult to express his deepest thoughts about being a *chueta*.

"The reality is that when I met you I thought that you fit right into Mallorca and knew you would understand my music," he wrote to me a few weeks after I left the island for France with the gift of a compact disc filled with his music.

I knew Bernat was preparing to travel to Israel in his eightieth year. He planned to submerge himself in the ritual bath of a *mikveh*—the culmination of years of study.

Instead, his children buried him. I was stunned to receive a note about his death in early December, a few months after his conversion the spring before. He had had so many plans. The local orchestra was going to perform his composition "Aquarius" in concert in February. He had told friends about his dream to move to Israel.

It was fitting, of course, that one memorial was held for

him at a local church in Palma, with a performance by his young students. His children organized a Jewish burial, where they read aloud a poem found on his table. It was written by the parent of one of his violin students, and he had been preparing to set it to music. It marked the twilight of Bernat's life, when he finally made peace with his ancestors.

"I carry a fragment of sea to the earth," the poem read in Catalan. "And with this sea inside me I will survive until the night of magic begins."

TWENTY-FOUR

Final Card

Lucainena de las Torres, Spain, August 2011

Sometimes the answers are in plain sight. How had I missed
them all? I kept pondering Rabbi Wiesel's clue about inexplicable family rituals, thinking about it in the desert in the
southeast of Spain. We were visiting another white Andalusian village, Lucainena de las Torres, on the outskirts of
the Sierra Alhamilla, where the blue nights lingered toward
midnight.

"Nowadays we have many, many people who look for the
truth, who look for an anchor in life," he told me. Perhaps
that's why I was so attracted to the bells of Arcos de la
Frontera and the ones tolling now above the plaza of this
tiny village of seven hundred people. The bells are my anchor.

They told me when to pray, celebrate, and flee. They marked my days. They invaded my nights.

I had the same dream about Santa María's bells, repeated again and again. In my dream, the bells are making the church shake, thundering through the dark nave. And I am sitting in a hard wooden pew, frozen in place, hypnotized by candle flames exploding into bonfires. The wooden doors are barred. The end is obvious.

I knew I had enough information to write our story. I knew that my family had shared the secret among the older generations that we were *sefarditas*, and that names, symbols, habits, and histories were part of the puzzle that answered my questions. Their histories had to be told or the memories would die. When stories die, we can't remember who we are or why we are here.

But I wanted a defining clue that resolved all doubts, much like the moment when I finally uncovered the meaning of the misspelled Latin inscription on the thick cup of the oldest bell in Arcos de la Frontera, the bell called La Nona, Grandmother. I had searched for answers through books of folklore and histories of bells.

Yet I finally unraveled the clandestine message with the help of the Museo de la Campana, the Bell Museum, in an old school in Meruelo, in a valley of northern Spain. The museum guarded the memories of when the region was the most important European hub for the production of bells, dating back to the fifteenth century. Its master founders crafted La

Gorda, which hangs in the cathedral of Toledo, and María for the cathedral in Pamplona.

The museum's collection of thirty-eight bells illustrated how the ancient founders played with messages on their masterworks, spelling out their thoughts in a mix of Latin and cryptic shorthand. One of its oldest bells, from 1574, helped me crack the code of the bell founder of Arcos de la Frontera and his mysterious message:

MENRTEN SANCTAM SPONTANEAM

HONOREM DEO PATI ET LIBERACIONEM

Most of the bells in the museum's collection are typically marked with a date along with a reference to God, Mary, and Joseph. But one of them contains another intriguing inscription: IHS MEN TEN SCTAN ES PONTA NE AN ONO REM DEO ET PA TRIE LI BERA TIONEM 1574.

It is shorthand for the same ancient expression that was misspelled on the Arcos bell with words like *"pati."* The inscription, according to the museum, has "an obscure meaning" that dates back to a third-century Christian martyr, Saint Agatha, in Catania, Sicily, who was venerated by Christians, pagans, and Jews because she protected the city from fire and volcanoes.

The legend is that after she spurned a Roman prefect, she was tortured and killed, and her body laid in a stone sarcophagus that was prepared for sealing. Then a young man, dressed in white silk, arrived with a hundred others. On the sarcophagus he placed a marble tablet, which bore the Latin abbreviation M.S.S.H.D.E.P.L., for the same expression, which means "Of sound and willing mind, honor God, homeland, and freedom."

The notion of defiance spread to Germany and England and Spain and became a charm to write on the ceiling or walls of a house for protection from lightning or fire. I like to think of it as a warning from the Arcos bell maker, Don Antón López, whose ringing message can be heard many ways. Cherish freedom. Honor God. Resist fire.

Why didn't my ancestors leave a message that also lingered? Their story always seemed to hover just over the edge of the horizon, a hidden homeland of secret resistance.

I know that some writers or biographers become consumed with the story they are tracking, tortured by the inability to settle questions. All I wanted was a scrap of paper. Words. Paragraphs.

I had talked to most of my relatives, shuffled through birth and death records, and tried to inhabit the past in many places. I was so close. In Costa Rica, my cousin Javier had offered more tantalizing clues about his grandmother, my great-aunt Luz. She told him her father was close friends with a rabbi, whom he visited often. In her bedroom dresser, Javier remembered, she kept a bronze menorah of seven branches, but she never explained its meaning.

And then he added one more thought. Aunt Luz always had dreams about returning to the region from which the

family came, the basin where the Guadalquivir and Guadalete rivers flow into the Gulf of Cádiz. I was amazed that she
was so precise.

Still, I yearned for something more. For a foundation to
rebuild an identity, something physical that I could hold. I
asked my cousin to find the menorah and to send me this
family totem or share photographs. While I waited, I kept
looking.

When I returned to our farmhouse in France, I started
searching for a mythical steamer trunk or battered carton
with clues to the past.

It was not the trunk. I had overlooked my antique walnut
secretary desk, footsteps from my bed. It was a wedding
present purchased in Lambertville, New Jersey, with money
from my grandmother Mamita. The secretary was filled with
the little detritus of assorted moves.

Within the slant-top desk, there were tiny shelves and
nooks with the flotsam of life, old Dutch guilder notes, a
sparkly pair of caramel cat-eye glasses from the fifth grade,
and a gold silhouette of a child's head from Mamita's charm
bracelet engraved with my name.

In one of the slots at the top were papers and cards that I
hadn't looked at for years, ever since the secretary desk had
traveled from the United States to France. I started rearrang-
ing all the documents on the shelves, tossing out Long Island
car insurance receipts from 1994 and a German bank account tally from 2001 that I would never need again.

I moved to the top slot and shuffled through holy cards

and newspaper clippings that my mother had sent me from California. They were all mementos of memories forgotten. And then I paused at a stiff, ivory-colored prayer card, passed out at funerals.

On one side was an embossed gold cross encircled in lilies, in memory of my great-aunt Luz Carvajal de Llubere, who died in October 1998 in San José, Costa Rica. On the other side of the card, was a prayer, Psalm 92.

> The righteous will flourish like a palm tree,
> They will grow like a cedar of Lebanon;
> planted in the house of the Lord,
> they will flourish in the temple of our God
> They will still bear fruit in old age.

I clasped my hand over my mouth in disbelief. Luz Carvajal, who had told others in the family that we were *sefarditas*, had gone to the grave with a traditional Sabbath prayer, the *shir shel yom*, "a psalm, a song for the day of Sabbath."

Just seeing the psalm with its reference to the temple made me laugh out loud with the pure pleasure of discovery and relief. Could this have been a Sabbath prayer adopted by Catholics? Perhaps. But given the great number of clues, including the menorah, I believed it was the missing piece of the puzzle. I was sure that great-aunt Luz, whose name means "light," had left a cryptic message.

It took me a mere thirteen years to decipher the little funeral card stashed in a drawer. Above it was the dark oil

painting of the mystic Santa Teresa de Ávila, her right hand
raised in warning and wreathed with pink roses that signified
secrets.

As I closed the hinged cover of the secretary desk, I shiv-
ered. Doubt was no longer my religion. For a fleeting moment
I could feel the hot *solano* winds. I could picture the massive
white Spanish sailing ship *Elcano* pressing through the heartbreaking blue waters of the Bay of Cádiz, where the Guadalete River spills. I carry the fragment of the sea within me.

The Carvajal family, photographed in the 1930s in San Jose, Costa Rica. Luz Carvajal, third from the left, standing, was the keeper of the family's secrets.

Epilogue

I am still searching for the bronze menorah that my great-aunt Luz stored in a commode in her garden apartment in San Jose, Costa Rica. I picture it as a worn object, dark and flecked green by time, touched by many hands. Maybe its markings offer clues to the secret lives of my ancestors.

I want to know the relationship between this object and my family. I can picture Luz's room where the menorah once was stored, remember the tiny space, the light from the window. I wonder what it witnessed?

One cousin remembers it vividly. Other relatives never saw it. Family history is jumbled like that. So is faith.

There are scientific studies that explore whether the experiences of our ancestors somehow become part of us, inherited in unexpected ways through a vast chemical network in our cells that controls our genetic makeup. At the heart of the field, known as epigenetics, is the notion that genes have memory and that the lives of our grandparents—what they breathed, saw, and ate—can directly affect us generations later.

French psychotherapist Anne Ancelin Schützenberger, now in her nineties and nearly blind, has spent decades studying what she calls the ancestor syndrome. She contends we are links in a chain of generations, unconsciously affected by their dramas and unfinished business until we acknowledge the past.

For the first generation, this family history is something unspoken, according to Ms. Schützenberger, who has worked in the field for five decades. For the second generation, it becomes a family secret. By the third and fourth generations, it lingers in the unconscious. She calls such history the "phantom in the crypt."

Recently, my cousin Rosie confided that she, too, had tried to raise the phantom. Many years ago, she recalled questioning Aunt Luz about our ancestry at a family gathering in Costa Rica. Given our family penchant for secrecy, she taped the conversation with a hidden recorder.

"Luz told me that our family came from Spain. She asked me, 'Has your mother ever told you that we are Sefarditas?'" Rosie said. "Of course, when I brought it up with my mother, she refused to talk."

It was after I had spoken to Rosie that I decided I needed a fresh approach. I had already done what Ms. Schützenberger had advised: I had immersed myself in what she calls the "ecological niche" of family—to walk in the footsteps of ancestors, exploring the history, geography, and economy of their times; eating their food; deciphering their grand cursive handwriting. I had tried to feel the pulse of the past.

It's a form of right-brain genealogy, making an emotional connection to ancestors. Family stories are like antiques, something revealed by rubbing old oak till it shines. But I still yearned for exactitude, for tough, hard facts that ended all doubts. I wanted a told-you-so moment.

In 2012 I was spurred on by the Spanish government's new offer of citizenship for the descendants of Sephardic Jews who had left Spain during the Inquisition. For proof, I re-examined my family tree, researching different lines that led to Spain. I had already hit a wall on the Carvajal family after discovering that my second great-grandfather had taken the name of his mother, Maria Carvajal. There was no document listing the father and I could not find more information about Maria.

This was a critical lesson in genealogy. I had stubbornly ignored other branches of the family tree. I was fixated on one name, Carvajal, but obviously there were many other ancestors. The solution came to me, curiously enough, while traveling in Madrid to visit the Royal Zarzuela Palace for a news profile of Spain's King Juan Carlos I.

As I settled into the formal palace sitting room—gazing at royal family photos and sterling-silver boxes engraved with the king's signature—I realized what I had to do: look in a new direction to the ancestry of my grandmother Angela Chacón.

I had assumed my grandmother was a Sephardic Jewish descendant because of the clannish way she was married off at seventeen into the Carvajal family when she was orphaned. But I wasn't sure.

New names emerged when I started working my way through Costa Rican baptismal certificates that were scanned and posted online. I was introduced to a distant great-grandfather, Álvaro de Acuña, a sixteenth-century conquistador who searched fruitlessly for El Dorado. There was also Leonora de Chacón de Narváez y Zapata, a wealthy colonist who left Andalusia with her family in 1603. Her husband, Juan de Alárcon de Rabaneda, was a Spanish judge who presided over arrests and property seizures. The family made it to the new world, but the judge died of a heart attack on the path to Costa Rica at the age of thirty-three. Their son drowned in a river.

Why did Leonora and Juan give up a life of privilege for a distant colony with no natural riches? I suspected, of course, that they were fleeing something, but I had no proof. Their names led me to genealogy journals in Central America with elaborate family trees of the early founders of Costa Rica that intersected with my own ancestral lines.

I collected the names mechanically, laying them aside for study later. One distant great-grandfather was Juan Vásquez de Coronado, a conquistador from Salamanca, Spain. At seventeen, he left for the new colonies and eventually became the governor of Costa Rica. Then he married a Spanish aristo-crat, Isabel Arias Dávila, daughter of a conquistador.

I studied the name of this ancestor that meant nothing to me. I had collected a pile of different books about the Inquisition to search for names. And every night I sat in the living room checking for clues. So the explosive moment, when it came, was actually solitary—though the chimes of an old French clock sounded midnight with sonorous notes.

The history books I read were were full of references to the Arias Dávila family who were pursued by the Inquisition even after their deaths. They were secret Jews prosecuted for heresy and "judaizing" in an Inquisition trial that explored their daily habits in meticulous detail. Their remains were secretly removed from Segovia in the fifteenth century and moved to Rome to avoid the public spectacle of an *auto-da-fé* when inquisitors could have burned their bones in effigy.

That night, sitting in the shadows of my living room, I understood at last the fear I inherited from generations of my ancestors. The trial was the most prominent investigation in the medieval history of Segovia, a public demonstration of the rising power of the Inquisition. Starting in 1486, Inquisitors gathered testimony from 231 witnesses for a trial three years later that targeted members of the Arias Dávila family.

They were wealthy *conversos* who struggled to remain Jews, split between two religions at the dawn of the Inquisition in 1478. Their patriarch was Diego Arias Dávila, my distant great-grandfather, who was born in 1380. His Jewish family converted to Christianity in 1411 in the tense period in

Segovia after the arrival of a fiery preacher named Vincent Ferrer. In a city that was once an important center of the Jewish community, Ferrer preached for the conversion of Jews and spread rumors that Jews had desecrated a communion host, leading to the execution of a Jewish physician.

Diego converted as a boy, discarding his name, Isaque Abenacar. Later he became the royal treasurer for two Spanish monarchs, Juan II de Castilla and his son Enrique IV. Yet he was so loathed for his efforts to raise taxes that a Spanish poet composed a bitter tribute: "Diego Arias, thou art a wretched hypocrite. A Jew thou wert and a Jew thou art. Great is the power that is thine. Hence to no dealings I incline."

In their daily lives, the family mixed identities. Diego Arias Dávila made donations to the Catholic church, but his wife, Elvira, also a convert at age eleven, helped fund construction of the Campo synagogue that still stands today.

Doña Elvira would secretly retreat to the communal *mikvah* for a ritual bath with Jewish relatives. Diego Arias Dávila yearned for the music of his childhood, gathering with Jewish friends in private to sing Hebrew melodies. They kept a kosher table and avoided going to mass.

Their son, Juan Arias Dávila, was the powerful bishop of Segovia for more than thirty years. Yet not even he could fend off the inquisitors of Tómas de Torquemada who targeted the Dávila family in a political clash with the bishop who also was accused of obstructing the Inquisition's work.

It was whispered that when Diego Arias Dávila and his

wife, Doña Elvira, were buried, their remains were prepared according to Jewish custom, wrapped in a cape and a hood. That was enough cause to provoke an investigation and posthumous Inquisition trial on twenty-three counts of "judaizing," or observing Jewish rituals in violation of their conversions.

Jews and Christians testified about the couple's most banal habits. Doña Elvira sent unleavened bread and lettuce to Jewish friends at Passover. On Saturdays she "idled" with Jews. The damning evidence also cited her passion for *adafina*, a Sephardic lamb stew, slow-cooked on embers and served for Sabbath lunch.

Some witnesses, though, scoffed that Diego Arias Dávila had faith in anything. The royal treasurer expressed doubts to others about salvation and an afterlife. But for good measure he purchased the entire chapel of a former monastery, La Merced, in 1461 as the site for a grand tomb.

The royal treasurer's joke about the location's double benefits emerged in the Inquisition record. It was a popular gathering spot, he told a friar. If the prayers of the monks didn't save him, then he had a second chance with the chants from a neighboring synagogue.

As the Inquisition's investigation proceeded, the bishop secretly disinterred his family's remains from their tomb and took refuge in Rome. From exile, he fought the Inquisition's accusations, fending off the charges without a record of a final ruling.

I tried in vain to find where the canny bishop hid the

remains of his parents and grandmother, Catalina Gonzalez. In Spain? Italy? Somewhere along the way? One day I would like to lay a rock on their tomb, a long-delayed tribute for sacrifices that lasted generations.

As I researched I began to feel a special connection to Doña Elvira. It was clear from the Inquisition testimony that she yearned to maintain the bonds of family, and the joys of taking pleasure in Jewish weddings and holidays. Those ties are so strong that she managed to share something precious with us sixteen generations later. Perhaps some things are meant to be.

I was startled when I discovered Doña Elvira's real name, which she changed after her conversion. She was originally called Clara. It's a strong name that means clear and bright. By coincidence—or maybe not—we named our daughter the French version, Claire.

Now it is my daughter's turn to shine bright.

ACKNOWLEDGMENTS

I am grateful to all who helped me on this journey that still continues. Many people in the town of Arcos de la Frontera gave me their time and the benefit of their wisdom. María Gómez Vásquez, widow of Manuel Pérez Regordán, generously allowed me access to the *cronista*'s library and any papers I cared to browse. Her son, José María Pérez, shared some of his reminiscences of his father and life in Arcos with me.

I am thankful for the aid of Mari Camarena and her husband, Pedro Carrera Caña, who invited me along on her own journey to reclaim her voice and the music of *saetas*. Many artists and poets in Arcos de la Frontera also shared their time and reflections with me, among them Manuel Gallardo Barroso, Antonio

Acknowledgments

Murciano, and Pedro Sevilla. My Arcos neighbor, María José Durán, shared something infinitely more practical: the poetry of friendship.

I am also indebted to a number of research institutions, among them the Bancroft Library at Berkeley and the Centro Andaluz de Flamenco in Jerez de la Frontera. Shavei Israel, the organization in Jerusalem, was also an enormous resource.

Many friends also came to my aid as test readers and sometimes as guides along the journey. Thanks to Dan Bilefsky for making me laugh and keeping me on track, and to Stephen Castle, who pressed me forward.

It was also my great fortune to benefit from the advice of my agent, Todd Shuster, who early on encouraged me to embark on a quest without knowing the result. Thanks also to my talented editor at Riverhead, Jake Morrissey, who had a gentle and thoughtful way of urging me onward, and to my long-time editor at *The New York Times*, Martin Gottlieb. I could not write a sentence without wondering what he would think, edit, or offer as a baseball analogy.

My family and my parents, Arnold and Carol, also have been a constant source of support—though I know that sometimes they were baffled by what exactly was happening on my quest. I hope that one day my daughter, Claire, who was also along for parts of the journey, will read this book and remember the generations before her. Finally, I want to say *merci* to my husband, Omer, who has contributed so much to this book— including long drives on perilous Spanish mountain roads, late nights at flamenco clubs, and many paella dinners. He will always be everything to me.

Doreen Carvajal is a Paris-based reporter for the *The New York Times* and the *International Herald Tribune*, covering European issues. She has been a journalist for more than twenty-five years and has reported on a broad range of subjects, from politics and immigration to book publishing and the media. She lives with her family near Paris.